Eighteenth Century Emigrants from Russheim in Baden-Durlach to the American Colonies

Researched and Compiled

By

Edward N. Wevodau

Grapevine, Texas

2018

Cover image: Philipsbourg "Carte de France" von Cassini, Nordosten (1763). Available via http://biblio.unibe.ch (University of Bern). Accessed via oldampsonline.

They came in groups.

Table of Contents

Russheim Evangelisch Church Records: 7
Emigrants from Russheim to the American Colonies..8
Russheimer Ships to America 11
American Colonial Immigrants from Russheim 14
Georg Albert 15
Leonhard Albert's Children (Peter Albert, Wilhelm Albert, and Margaretha Albert) 20
Elisabeth Becher 22
Georg Braun (and possibly his brother Adam Braun) 26
Georg Ulrich Britz 28
Joseph Burgstahler 30
Elser (or Eltzer) Family 33
Catharina Barbara Gangwolff 38
Christoph Hacker & sons Hans Adam Hacker and Johann Georg Hacker 40
Johann Adam Haushalter and siblings 43
Lorentz Haushalter 47
Martin Jock (or Jogg)..50
Wendel Keller 53
Diebold Lang and his son Michael Lang 55
Veit Müller..61
Adam Nees and his son Johannes Nees 63
Michael Nees 67
Sebastian Nees (or Neess) 70
Johannes Seitz...73
Barbara Schmidt (Widow of Friedrich Schmidt)..76
Martin Schmidt 78
Johann Adam Speck and Bernhard Speck 80
Martin Speck (or Spöck) 82
Friederich Werner 84
Catharina Zimmerman and her sons Johann Friederich, Johann Michael, and Johannes Zimmerman.......85
Other Russheim Emigrants Identified by Hacker 87
Recommended Resources 89

Local History 89
Addendum: Russheim Hager Family 92
Notes on Sources 94
Index of Surnames 104

Modern Germany identification:

Dettenheim, Landkreis Karlsruhe, State of Baden-Württemberg, Bundesrepublik Deutschland

(or Dettenheim, Karlsruhe, Baden-Württemberg, Germany)

Postal Code: 76706 Dettenheim

In the eighteenth century, several waves of emigrants left the German village of Russheim for the American Colonies. All first settled in Pennsylvania. For generations, Russheimers lived in close proximity to each another in modern-day Lancaster and Lebanon counties.

Today, the former village of Russheim (or Rußheim, as written with traditional German characters) is part of the municipality of Dettenheim (once briefly called Liedolsheim-Russheim), in Landkreis Karlsruhe in Baden-Württemberg.

This work attempts to document all known and probable emigrants from Russheim to British Colonial America in the eighteenth century.

Source: Landkreis Karlsruhe (German Wikipedia)

How emigrants were identified:

1. Werner Hacker's *Auswanderung aus Baden und dem Breisgau*. Professor Hacker searched German archives for evidence of migration. Legally, a German who intended to depart for American had to apply for permission to emigrate (called manumission)—a process by which taxes and other matters could be resolved or addressed. Professor Hacker compiled his findings in a series of publications. In the United States, Closson Press has published an index to his collected works entitled *Eighteenth Century Register of Emigrants from Southwest Germany*. I own a copy of *Auswanderung aus Baden und dem Breisgau*, which covers the region in which Russheim is located. Using the place name index in the back of the book. I compiled all identified emigrants from Russheim in the eighteenth century who intended to depart for the American Colonies.
2. Passenger Lists. All ships arriving at the Port of Philadelphia had to provide a list of all non-British citizens aboard. These immigrants were then administered the Oath of Allegiance to the British Crown, at which time they signed their names to document. Generally, family units and persons who had traveled together stood in line together. When an emigrant from Russheim was identified on a passenger list, I searched all names written above and below in the village church books.
3. American Colonial Records. I searched for evidence of the Russheimers in America, compiling all significant findings. When the evidence connected the Russheimer to other persons, I investigated the origins of those persons. Germans tended to travel in groups. They departed their homeland together and then settled in America together. In the records compiled below, American baptismal sponsors for the children of Russheimers were often from either Russheim it or neighboring villages (e.g., Graben, Linkenheim, and Eggenstein).
4. Russheim Evangelisch Church records. I viewed the original Russheim Evangelisch church records, which are available via digitized microfilm on the website Archion.de. A few notices of emigration were noted by the pastor.
5. Databases and websites. I used general keyword searches (e.g., "Russheim" + Pennsylvania) to locate websites with information related to possible migrations. The websites Ancestry and FamilySearch were used to seek evidence of other researchers who had located eighteenth century emigrants from Russheim. I consulted my personal library collection, which has a special emphasis on works related to eighteenth century German emigration.

IMPORTANT: This work should not be considered comprehensive. Not all emigrants applied for manumission. The church pastor did not typically identify those who left the congregation. For example: 1754 emigrant Bernhard Speck was identified only by his marriage record in the Lancaster Lutheran church books, which gave his former residence as Russheim. He later appears as a baptismal sponsor for 1752 emigrant Adam Speck, who did apply for manumission. Only by researching the web of relationships in both German and America were some emigrants identified. Surely others were missed.

In creating this file, I pursued only eighteenth century emigrants from this village. I saw evidence of quite a few emigrants in the nineteenth century

CAVAET: I personally compiled all records cited below from the original Russheim Evangelisch church books. This work represents my initial effort at reading old-style German script. I am a beginner—and my translations are subject to error. If these records identify a direct ancestor, I encourage you to access and view the original records on your own to verify the dates and information. I am comfortable navigating basic entries, but when the pastor added unique facts or notes, I often struggled. If I could not read information of possible importance, I copied the original record and indicated my difficulty.

I will also add that several of the pastors at Russheim had poor handwriting; further, some pages of the digitized microfilm were too dark to read. Reading this book requires a high degree of skill. I learned much—but I am not a professional German researcher. Be advised!

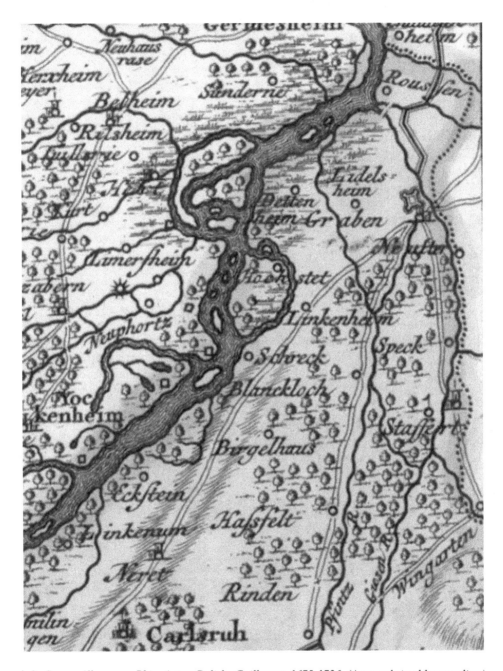

Le Flambeau de la Guerre Allumee au Rhin. Autor: Delisle, Guillaume, 1675-1726. (Accessed via oldmapsonline.)

Scores of emigrants left Baden-Durlach (colored blue in the map above) for America in the eighteenth century. On the map, Russheim is spelled Rousen. Other villages pictured with documented emigrants: Liedolsheim, Hochstetten, Graben, Linkenheim, Schröck, Spöck, Staffort, Blankenloch, Berghausen, Hagsfeld, Rintheim, Eggenstein, and Neureut.

RUSSHEIM EVANGELISCH CHURCH RECORDS:

Digitized images of the Russheim Evangelisch Church records can be found on the website Archion.de. With a paid subscription, the images may be accessed, downloaded, and printed. I consulted the following digitized books:

Russheim Evangelisch Church Records, 1692-1738:

Baptisms (1692-1731): Bild 1
Marriages: Bild 54
Communicants: Bild 66
Death Register: Bild 83
Baptisms (1731-1738): Bild 114

Russheim Evangelisch Church Records, 1738-1777:

Baptisms (1738-1777): Bild 1
Deaths (1738-1817): Bild 107 to Bild 235 [index last five pages]
Marriages (1738-1800): Bild 236

In early 2016, Ancestry added a database entitled *Baden, Germany, Lutheran Baptisms, Marriages, and Burials, 1502-1985*. The Evangelisch Register of Russheim appears in this database. Users can search for ancestors using various keyword searches and filters. The page in the original church book is given. Due to the difficulty of reading the original record, expect that not all indexed surnames appear correctly.

All clippings of original records used in this monograph were acquired via Archion.de. I verified all abstracted records in the original book. I encourage direct descendants of Russheimers to subscribe to Archion and access the original records of their ancestors. More information may be found in the original records than I include in this monograph.

EMIGRANTS FROM RUSSHEIM TO THE AMERICAN COLONIES

In his work entitled *Auswanderung aus Baden und dem Breisgau*. Professor Werner Hacker identified emigrants from Russheim. I investigated all emigrants who may have departed for British Colonial America.

#	Russheim Emigrant	Year	Destination	Ship
38	Albert, Joh. Georg	1737	America	1737 Molly
39	Albert, Peter und Wilhelm	1752	Unknown	1752 Phoenix
467	Becher, Elisabeth	1737	Unknown	
957	Boltz, Christina	1752	Unknown	
1065	Braun, Adam	1747	Unknown	
1072	Braun, Georg	1752	America	1752 Rawley
1159	Britz, Ulrich	1749	America	
1874	Elser, Margarete	1749	America	1749 Anna
2614	Gangolff, Catharina Barbara	1749	America	
3384	Hager, Margarete	1749	America	
3385	Hager, Catharine	1749	America	
3405	Hacker, Christof	1752	America	1752 Rawley
3653	Hausser, Lorenz	1752	America	1752 Rawley
3775	Haushalter, Johann	1739	America	1739 Friendship
3776	Haushalter, Lorenz	1752	America	1752 Rawley
4623	Jock, Martin	1737	America	1739 Friendship
5985	Lang, Hans Michael	1752	America	1752 Rawley
7274	Neff [sic: Nees], Michael	1744	America	1737 William
7290	Nees, Joh. Michael	1737	America	1737 William
7291	Nees, Joh. Adam	1749	America	1749 Ann
8168	Roth, Lorenz	1768	Unknown	
8408	Seitz, Johann	1752	America	1752 Rawley
9125	Schmidt, Martin	1737	America	
9129	Schmidt, Joh. Georg	1737	Unknown	
9137	Schmid, Barbara	1749	America	1749 Ann
9650	Speck, Martin	1737	America	1738 Friendship
9652	Speck, Barbara	1749	America	1749 Ann
9653	Speck, Johann Adam	1752	America	1752 Phoenix
10768	Weber, Michael	1737	America	
10789	Weber, Burkhard	1755	Unknown	
11089	Winacher [sic: Reinacher], Margarete	1737	America	
11380	Zimmermann, Catharine	1749	America	1749 Ann

#	Russheim Emigrant	Hacker Notes
38	Albert, Joh. Georg	see Hacker for more: frau Marg Weinacker od. Reinacher
39	Albert, Peter und Wilhelm	brothers; with Stiefvater Adam Speck
467	Becher, Elisabeth	widow; planned to accompany Johann Haushalter and Martin Jock
957	Boltz, Christina	widow; with daughter Maria Margaretha, age 14
1065	Braun, Adam	deserted Russheim
1072	Braun, Georg	with wife and one child
1159	Britz, Ulrich	with wife and five children
1874	Elser, Margarete	A widow; born Hager; to Pennsylvania with Mock from Graben
2614	Gangolff, Cath. Barb.	Mother is the widow of the Schultheissen
3384	Hager, Margarete	see Hacker 1874--same person
3385	Hager, Catharine	widowed Zimmermann, deren Kdr erwachsen sind, darf nach Pennsylvania
3405	Hacker, Christof	Schuster
3653	Hausser, Lorenz	also known as Lorentz Haushalter; see Hacker 3776
3775	Haushalter, Johann	his 1737 application for manumission was rejected
3776	Haushalter, Lorenz	with frau
4623	Jock, Martin	his 1737 application for manumission was rejected
5985	Lang, Hans Michael	With wife and 2 children.; Glechzeitig Chr Hacker
7274	Neff [sic: Nees], Michael	Er und Mtin Weidmann von Graben beide in Lancaster Pennsylvania an sich gezogen haben Erbteil der
		Marg Winacher (?Reinacher) husband of Gg Albert
7290	Nees, Joh. Michael	to Pennsylvania
7291	Nees, Joh. Adam	with wife and four children
8168	Roth, Lorenz	his destination was not indicated
8408	Seitz, Johann	with wife and three children
9125	Schmidt, Martin	took 450 florins with him
9129	Schmidt, Joh. Georg	with wife and five children; with father Martin; refiled 1738
9137	Schmid, Barbara	geboren Speck, with mdrjahrigen Kdrn; see Emigrant 9652
9650	Speck, Martin	
9652	Speck, Barbara	vw (widow of) Schmid, mit mdrjahrigen Kdrn; more info in Hacker
9653	Speck, Johann Adam	wife and two children
10768	Weber, Michael	to Pennsylvania
10789	Weber, Burkhard	his destination was not indicated

11089	Winacher [sic: Reinacher], Margarete	husband Georg Alberts, in Pennsylvania, lasst von dort dch Bevollmachtigten Melch Kuhner aus dem Saarbrucken;
		see also Hacker 10665; jetz in Lancaster, Pennsylvania (1748)
11380	Zimmermann, Catharine	geboren Hager; a widow

Of significance:

Smith, Clifford Neal, trans. *Emigrants from the West-German Fuerstenberg Territories (Baden and the Palatinate) to America and Central Europe, 1712, 1737, 1787.* (German-American Genealogical Research Monograph Number 9.) McNeal, Arizona: Westland Publications, 1981. (Reprinted by the Genealogical Publishing Co., Inc., in Baltimore, Maryland, in 2004.)

In his forward, Mr. Smith explains his work as a translation Herman Baier's 1937 published research. Herr Baier had examined emigration from the aforesaid territories in the years 1712, 1737, and 1787. The years were chosen, Mr. Neal explains, for reasons of historical significance.

All but one person identified as from Russheim in this translation was also identified in Professor Werner Hacker's work; however, on rare occasions, this book provides details are provided that Professor Hacker did not include in *Auswanderungen aus Baden und dem Breisgau*.

The person identified in Clifford Neal Smith's translation, but omitted by Hacker, is as follows:

Friedrich Werner of Russheim, manumitted 1737. Intends to go to America.

RUSSHEIMER SHIPS TO AMERICA

Strassburger and Hinke's *Pennsylvania German Pioneers* was used to identify immigrants. I found emigrants from Russheim on the ships below. The persons underlined are documented in this work. All persons signed their names unless indicated by a mark placed in parentheses.

The order of names is the same as the order of signers on List B as transcribed and published in *Pennsylvania German Pioneers*. If a name appears on List A but not List B then I inserted it and made notice. An ellipsis indicates a series of names was omitted by this compiler.

I included other passengers in order to give a sense of how emigrants from these villages tended to group themselves together.

Snow *Molly*, qualified 10 Sep 1737 at Philadelphia:

Veltin Stober
Valentin Stober, Junior
Jacob Stober
Hans Jonas Reiffel
Friederich Reiffel
Johan Christoff Grohmann
Johann Albrecht Schaller
Johann Georg Albrecht (surname given as Albert on List A)
Georg Albrecht Schaller

Ship *William*, qualified 31 Oct 1737 at Philadelphia:

Jacques Creucas
Mathias Schmidt
Johan Michel Neess
Theobald (X) Lange
Johan Peter Wilms
Jacob Heinrich Weidtmann
Johannes Weydtmann

Ship *Friendship*, qualified 20 Sep 1738 at Philadelphia:

Valentin Schaller, age 24
Michel Karcher, age 46
Hans Jörg Becher, age 18
Johannes Kuhn, age 30
Debalt Klingler, age 24
…..
Fridrig Karle, age 26
Sebastian (X) Neas, age 55

Henrich Hernner, age 46
Geo. Daniel (X) Gesmer, age 45
Veit Bechtoldt, age 26
…...
Johan Martin Karcher, age 19
Daniel Friedrich Reinekh, age 32
Hans Enger (X) Bough, age 40 (Hans Jurg Buck on List A)
Dedrich (FH) Hilie, age 20 (Fredrich Haylie on List A—probably Frederick Hahnle/Hainle)
<u>Martin (+) Speck, age 35</u>
Hans Georg Konig, age 30
Johan Wendel Braun, age 37

Ship *Friendship*, qualified 3 Sep 1739 at Philadelphia:
Frantz Brossman, age 45
Michael (X) Floris [not in this position on List A]
<u>Veit Miller, age 25</u>
Christian (X) Ergott, age 25
Henrich Heyl, age 40
……..
Johan Veit Benner, age 22 (appears as John [H] Fybaylor on List B)
<u>Martin (O) Yoak, age 31</u>
John Philip (+) Herberger
<u>Johan Adam ([) Housholter, age 20</u>
Johan Nicolaus Maurer, age 23 (signed his name)
--Signed next to each other.

Ship *Ann*, qualified 28 Sep 1749 at Philadelphia:
Adam Schaulling
Daniel Scheübly
<u>Henrich Mock</u>
<u>Petter Elser</u>
<u>Hans Adam Hacker</u>
Johann Jacob (X) Sutz
Michel Hengsd [sic]
Jean Thoulouzan
Johannes Weber
Johanes Strauwman
Jacob Landgraff
<u>Johann Friedrich Zimmerman</u>
<u>H. Michael Zimmerman</u>
<u>Johanis Zimmerman</u>
Thomas ( ) Lubek, sick
<u>Wendel (WK) Keller</u>
….
<u>Hans Adam Nees</u>
<u>Hans Nes</u>

Ship *Rawley*, qualified 23 Oct 1752 at Philadelphia:

Hans Jerg Steidinger
Johan Philip (X) Frech
George (X) Brown
Johannes Seitz
Lorentz (X) Houshalter
Joseph Burgstahler
Christoph Hacker
Michel Lang
Matheas (X) Miller
Hans Jorg Mock
Hans Jorg Wächter
--All signed next to each other.

Ship *Phoenix*, qualified 22 Nov 1752 at Philadelphia:

Johann Adam Speck (signed his name)
Johann Georg Jeck (signed his name)
....
Wilhelm (X) Albert
--Signed some distance apart.

Ship *Henrietta*, qualified 22 Oct 1754 at Philadelphia:

Bernhard Speck

American Colonial Immigrants from Russheim

Each of the emigrants below was investigated in both German and Colonial American records. I included the most relevant information found. Some of the emigrants are certain—with direct evidence available. Others are identified only through circumstantial reasoning.

Emigrant	Year	Ship	Pennsylvania Residence
Albert, Georg	1737	Molly	Berks County
Albert, Wilhelm	1752	Phoenix	
Albert, Peter	1752		
Becher, Georg	1738	Friendship	
Boltz, Christina	1752		
Braun, Georg	1752	Rawley	Lancaster County
Britz, Georg Ulrich	1749	Ann	Philadelphia County
Burgstahler, Joseph	1752	Rawley	
Elser, Adam heirs	1749	Ann	Lancaster County
Mock, Henrich	1749	Ann	Lancaster County
Gangwolff, Catharina Barbara	1748		
Hacker, Adam	1749	Ann	Lancaster County
Hacker, Christoph	1752	Rawley	Lancaster County
Hacker, Georg	1751	Brothers	Philadelphia County
Haushalter, Adam	1739	Friendship	Lancaster County
Haushalter, Lorentz	1752	Rawley	Lancaster County
Jock, Martin	1739	Friendship	Lancaster County
Keller, Wendel	1749	Ann	Lancaster County
Lang, Diebold	1737	William	Berks County
Lang, Michael	1752	Rawley	Lancaster County
Neess, Michael	1737	William	Lancaster County
Muller, Veit	1739	Friendship	Lancaster County
Neess, Sebastian	1738	Friendship	Lancaster County
Neess, Adam	1749	Ann	
Neess, Hans	1749	Rawley	
Seitz, Johannes	1752	Rawley	Berks County
Schmidt, Martin	1738		
Speck, Martin	1738	Friendship	Lancaster County
Speck, Adam	1752	Phoenix	Lancaster County
Speck, Bernhard	1754	Henrietta	Lancaster County
Zimmerman, Frederick	1749	Ann	Lancaster County
Zimmerman, Michael	1749	Ann	Lancaster County
Zimmerman, Johannes	1749	Ann	Lancaster County

Georg Albert

1737 Molly

Georg Albert and his wife Margaretha Reinacher left a remarkable trail of records that prove their German origins.

Margaretha first married Martin Hörner, who died in 1729 at Russheim. Their daughter Maria Christina Hörner came to America with her mother and stepfather; however, their younger daughter Maria Catharina, died 28 Aug 1738 at Russheim—more than a year after the parents emigrated. I have difficulty reading Maria Catharina's burial record (see below), which makes mention that her mother had gone to Pennsylvania.

Perhaps documents sits in a German archive that may shed light on the circumstances.

GERMAN RECORDS:

Russheim Evangelisch KB:

Married 8 Apr 1704: Johannes Rheinnacher, son of Friedrich Rheinnacher, and Anna Catharina Karchen, daughter of Lorentz Karchen

Johannes Reinacher (or Rheinacher) & his wife Catharina had baptized:
1. Maria Margaretha, born 14 Feb 1706, baptized 14 Feb 1706
2. Anna Catharina, born 31 Mar 1709, baptized 1 Apr 1709
3. Johann Jacob, born 27 Oct 1712, baptized 28 Oct 1712
4. Anna Christina, born 26 Nov 1717, baptized 28 Nov 1717

Johann Martin Hörner & his wife Margaretha, born Reinacher, had baptized:
1. Christina, born 24 Aug 1726, sp. Lorenz Mainzer of Liedolsheim (and others)
2. Catharina Elisabetha, born 30 Sep 1727, baptized 2 Oct 1727, sp. Lorentz Maintzer of Liedolsheim and Michael Wächter of Liedolsheim (and others)
3. Maria Catharina, born 22 June 1729 ("filia posthuma")—died 29 Aug 1738; baptismal sponsor was Lorentz Maintzer of Liedolsheim

Note: No marriage record for this couple located in the Russheim records. Two Margaretha Reinacher's of the right age were born in Russheim.

Died 1 June 1729: Martin Horner, aged 29 years, 2 months, 27 days (also a short obituary)

Married 3 Nov 1733: Johann Georg Albert, the son of Wilhelm Albert, of Eschau im dem Hochgraff Erbachschen, and Margaretha, the widow of Martin Hörner, former citizen and master baker

Johann Georg Albert & his wife Margaretha had baptized:
1. Maria Eva, born 1 Aug 1734, baptized 2 Aug 1734—died 2 May 1737

Below: 1738 Burial record for Maria Catharina Hörner, daughter of Martin Hörner. The image exposure on the microfilm is difficult to read. In the middle of the image is the surname "Albrechtin." Surrounding text (not show) indicates the child's mother next married.....and went...." I believe the word "land" is the far left. The child's mother would have been in Pennsylvania at the time of her daughter's death—though I cannot read all the words, the pastor must be indicating such.

Landeskirchliches Archiv Karlsruhe > Rußheim > Mischbuch 1692 - 1738 - Bild 113

IMMIGRATION:

Hacker, *Auswanderung aus Baden und dem Breisgau:*

Hacker Emigrant 38:
Joh. Georg Albert, burger, Russheim, to Pennsylvania, manumitted 13 Feb 1737. Addendum 23 July 1748: Lately of Lancaster in Pennsylvania. Wife Margaret Weinecker ord. Reinacher. Melchior Kühner of Saarland to receive on her behalf hereditary property. (Note: Hacker identifies emigrant as Joh. Michael Albert—I believe this to be a transcription error.)

Hacker Emigrant 11089:
Margarete Winacher [sic: Reinacher], Russheim, wife of Georg Albert in Pennsylvania. "Lasst von dort dch Bevollmachtigten Melch Kuhner aus dem Saarbrücischen in Pennsylvania ihr Erbvmandfordern, das Michael Neff, Russheim, und Martin Weiseman, Graben,--beide jetzt in Lancaster—an sich gezogen haben. Dated 23 July 1748. (Melchior Kuhner of Saarbrucken is her legal representative to acquire her hereditary estate in Germany. She now lives in Lancaster, Pennsylvania. Michael *Neess* and Martin *Weidmann* were other Baden-Durlach emigrants. They appear to be her legal representatives in Pennsylvania.)

Snow *Molly*, qualified 10 Sep 1737 at Philadelphia:

Johan Christoff Grohmann
Johann Albrecht Schaller
<u>Johann Georg Albrecht</u> (surname given as Albert on List A)
Georg Albrecht Schaller

Note: I have some doubts as to whether this is Georg Albert of Russheim. The surnames Albert and Albrecht can be interchanged in records, but the Russheim immigrant's name is Albert on all other occasions. But I see no other possibility in Strassburger and Hinke's transcribed passenger lists. The Snow Molly did have passengers from other German villages near to Russheim.

PENNSYLVANIA RECORDS:

Berks County, Pennsylvania, Estate Files:

George Albert, 1753, Reading (family search image 80;
1. Contains last will and testament in German and also in English.
2. Inventory dated 9 July 1754: One stone house messuage or tenement and lot of ground situate in the town of Reading, marked in the General Plan of the town No. 35. Also two out lots of grounds, No. 7 and No. 63. Mentions items in the custody of Martin Cast and his wife Margaret, the late widow of George Albert.
3. Several accounts, including one for payments for the completion of buildings begun in the life time of the said George Albert and finished by Martin Cost.
4. Orphans Court documented dated 2 Sep 1754: Eve Albert, son of the daughters of George Albert, deceased, about 14 years of age, requests that Abraham Brosius of Reading be appoint her guardian. (Done) At the same time, George Albert, son of the said George Albert, desired that William Hottenstein be appointed his guardian. (Done)

Berks Will A5:
George Albert of Reading, writ 19 Nov 1752, probated 25 July 1753
1. "with great sickness and weakness in Body"
2. "The three children now at hand shall have shares alike."
3. To his young son: The stone house in Reading.
4. All the estate shall remain in the possession of the wife Margreta until after her decease—but that is if she continues a widow. If she shall be married again, then the estate shall be divided between the children and the wife according to the written law of the Province.
5. The daughter who is not married—Eva—shall have her portion when she is married as the other daughter when she was married.
6. The daughter Eva shall have the new Bible and the book called Stepp Const (?), and the young son George shall have the old Bible.
7. But if the daughter Christina should receive any portion on her side from Germany the same shall be added to the present estate and divided by equal shares among the children.
8. The saw mill which is built for the son-in-law should be valued unto him for 20 pounds Pennsylvania money. Christina did also receive 10 pounds lent money, together 30 pounds, which shall be made good to the two young children. The son-in-law shall be obliged to give a passable bond for his 30 pounds.
9. Signed his name with the mark IA.
10. Witnessed by Johan George Yok and Alexander Klinger. (Note: The surname Jock appears in Russheim and several emigrants of this surname came to the Americas.)
11. Testament spoken to Peter Snider, Philip Jacob Myer, and Abraham Brosius.

Berks Deed 4-197: Peter Withington, innholder, & his wife Eve of Cumru Township rel.to George Albert, yeoman, of the Town of Reading
    --Their right & title to Lot No. 35 in the Town of Reading, including all messuages and tenements: HISTORY: Lot No. 35 in the Town of Reading patented 7 Feb 1752 to George Albert, the

elder (Ref. Patent A-18-1). By his last will & testament, George Albert devised the same to his son George, the second party hereto. However, the wording of the testament only indicated the property as an estate for life whereas the intent was to invest an estate in fee Simple in his son George. At the time of the decease, the testator had only issue the said George and the said Eve, now wife of Peter Withington.
 --7 June 1765

Warwick Lutheran KB, Warwick Township, Lancaster County, Pennsylvania:

Signers of the 1743 Warwick Congregation Church Doctrine:
Johann Georg Albert

Joh. Georg Albert had baptized:
1. Eva Christina, born 8 Oct 1739, baptized 21 Oct 1739, sp. Joh. Valentin Stober; Joh. Martin Oberlin & Eva Jelterin
2. Joh. Georg, born 13 Mar 1744, baptized 14 Mar 1744, sp. Martin Weidtmann; Martin Oberlin & Barbara Süssin

Joh. Georg Albert & his wife Margaretha sponsored child of Martin Weidtmann on 12 Nov 1738
Joh. Georg Albert & his wife Margaretha sponsored two children of Peter Jelter on 8 Apr 1739
Joh. Georg Albert & his wife Margaretha and Joh. Michael Beyerle, Jr., sponsored child of Joh. Martin Oberlin on 16 Oct 1743 and 24 Mar 1745 (Note: Michael Beyerle, Jr., married to Anna Maria at the second baptism)

Balthasar Süss, Margaretha Albertin, and Margaretha Eichelbergerin sponsored child of Joh. Georg Eichelberger on 6 Oct 1745

Joh. Georg Albert & his wife sponsored child of Valentin Stober on 27 Mar 1748

Peter Wolffssperger & Christina Hörnerin sponsored child of Paul Hammerich on 26 June 1743
Christoph Süss and Maria Christina Hörnerin sponsored child of Joh. Georg Eichelberger on 25 Mar 1744

Note: Christina Hörnerin was the stepdaughter of Johann Georg Albert.

Stoever, Rev. John Casper, personal register:

Maria Christina Hoerner married 15 Mar 1748 David Zeller

Reading Lutheran KB, Berks County, Pennsylvania:

Maria Margaretha Kast, widow of Martin Kast. Born 25 Mar 1705 in Russheim in Durlach, the daughter of Johannes Reinacher & his wife Catharina. Married three times. Died 2 Oct 1775, aged 70 years, 6 months, 1 week Buried Oct. 4, 1775

Wife of Martin Kast. Born in the village of Russheim; daughter of Johann Reinacher and Catharina, his wife; Baptized soon after birth. While still in her native land she was married to Martin Herner with whom she lived about 4 years and 6 months when he died. She had 3 daughters by him, one of them still living. 5 years thereafter she was married to Georg Albert, with whom she came to this country and settled in this town. She lived with him 19 years and bore him 8 children. Only one son and one daughter survive. Having again become a widow, after 3 months, she married the present husband (Kast) with whom she lived 22 years and 6 months. She leaves 3 children and 19 grandchildren.

(Source: Burials, during the pastorate of Joh. Christf. Hadwig, of the Trinity Lutheran Church, Reading, Berks Co., Pa.)

Leonhard Albert's Children (Peter Albert, Wilhelm Albert, and Margaretha Albert)

Three of Leonhard Albert's children by his first wife went to America. This Leonhard Albert may be related to Georg Albert (q.v.) of Russheim.

GERMAN RECORDS:

Russheim Evangelisch KB:

Married 26 Jan 1723: Leonhard Albert, citizen and wagner at Schonau im Grafschaft Erbach, and Anna Catharina Wernerin, daughter of the ------ (omitted) Werner, citizen of Russheim.

Leonhard Albert & his wife Anna Catharina had baptized:
1. Margaretha, born 7 Jan 1724, baptized 9 Jan 1724
2. Mara Barbara, born 12 Jan 1725—died 8 Mar 1736
3. Johannes, born 27 May 1726 –died 24 Oct 1726
4. Maria Elisabetha, born 11 Sep 1729—died 19 Jan 1732
5. Johann Peter, born 11 Aug 1732, baptized 15 Aug 1732
6. Maria Catharina, born 11 Aug 1732, baptized 15 Aug 1732—died 25 Mar 1743
7. Wilhelm, born 17 Sep 1734

Died 23 Mar 1736: Anna Catharina, born Wernerin, legitimate wife of Leonhard Albert, aged 32 years, 2 months, 3 days

----

Married 2 Oct 1736: Leonhard Alberth, a widower, and Catharina Ulmerin, daughter of Hans Adam Ulmer

Leonhart Albert & his wife Catharina, nee Ulmer, had baptized:
1. Maria Eva, born 19 Oct 1737, baptized 20 Oct 1737
2. Johann Michael, born 11 Nov 1740, baptized 13 Nov 1740
3. Catharina Christina, baptized 13 May 1743—died 29 Dec 1748
4. Johannes, baptized 20 Mar 1745—died 26 Mar 1745
5. Maria Barbara, born 20 Jan 1747, baptized 20 Jan 1747—died 22 Apr 1782
6. Susanna, born 4 Dec 1748, baptized 4 Dec 1748—died 5 June 1807

Died 18 Dec 1748: Johan Leonard Albert, citizen and wagner, aged 47 years

Died 19 Oct 1783: Catharina Albert, born Ulmerin, the widow of Leonhard Albert, citizen and wagner, aged 71 years, 11 months

Married 7 Feb 1747: Johannes Seitz, citizen and tailor, son of Martin Seitz, and Margaretha Albertin, daughter of Leonhart Albert. They had baptized:
1. Catharina Elisabetha, born 14 Dec 1747
2. Catharina Barbara, born 5 Mar 1750
3. Christina, born 25 Oct 1751 (Pastor's notation: "went to the new land")

--See the section on the Seitz family for additional information. They arrived at Philadelphia aboard the Ship Rawley in 1752.

IMMIGRATION:

Hacker, Prof. Werner. *Auswanderungen aus Baden und dem Breisgau.*

Emigrant 39: Albert (Gebrüder) Peter u. Wilhelm, led Bgrsöhne, Russheim, Stiefvater JAdam Speck, Vm 42 fl. Mm. 1752. (Interpretation: Brothers Peter Albert and Wilhelm Albert of Russheim manumitted with their stepfather Johann Adam Speck.)

Caveat: I could locate no evidence exists that an Adam Speck married a Widow Albert. The widow of Leonhard Albert died in Russheim in 1783. See the section on the Speck, or Spöck, family for additional information.

Ship *Brothers*, qualified 16 Sep 1751 at Philadelphia:
Christof Weber
Georg Hacker
Peter Abert (sic: Albert?)
Johannes Schmitt
--Above: Georg Hacker was an emigrant from Russheim. Is that Peter Albert, son of Leonhard Albert, signing next to him? If so, his arrival conflicts with the date of his manumission.

Ship *Phoenix*, qualified 22 Nov 1752 at Philadelphia:

Johann Adam Speck (signed his name)
Johann Georg Jeck (signed his name)
....
Wilhelm (X) Albert
--Signed some distance apart.

AMERICAN COLONIAL RECORDS:

I did locate persons in American records who—in probability—were the Russheim emigrants Peter Albert and Wilhelm Albert. The Peter Albert who arrived in 1751 appears to have lived in Berks County in 1768 and later moved to Mahanoy Township, Northumberland County.

Their sister Margaretha Seitz, wife of Johannes Seitz (q.v.), settled in Berks County, Pennsylvania.

Elisabeth Becher

An Elisabeth Becher, widow, applied for manumission in 1737, along with Johann Haushalter and Martin Jock. The requests of all three were denied. Johann Haushalter and Martin Jock later arrived at Philadelphia in 1739. Did Elisabeth Becher continue with them?

In 1738, the Ship *Friendship* arrived in Philadelphia carrying a few persons whose origin can be traced to Russheim. A Hans Jörg Becher, age 18, signed the passenger list. The age and spelling of the surname match that of a child of Georg Becher, schoolmaster, and his wife Anna Elisabeth of Russheim. However, a caveat: This immigrant Becher did not sign his name near to other Russheim emigrants.

The information below is presented for consideration.

Russheim burial records were checked to the end of the year 1820. Georg Becher's widow Anna Elisabeth does not appear. Nor does their son Georg Becher. Marriage records were also checked to the end of the year 1770. The only persons of this surname who appear in the church records post-1735 are members of the Christoph Adam Becher family. This man was a son of the said Georg Becher by an earlier wife.

.

GERMAN RECORDS:

Russheim Evangelisch KB:

Died 30 Nov 1705: Johannes, sons of Hans Jerg Becher, schoolmaster here, aged 5 (?) days

Died 8 Dec 1705: Magdalena Catharina, wife of Hans Jerg Becker, schoolmaster here, aged 37 years, 8 months, and 29 days.

Married 18 May 1706: Johann Georg Becker, widower and schoolmaster here, and Anna Elisabetha, the daughter of Stephan Hacker, citizen and Schneider here

Joh. Jerg Becher, schoolmaster, & his wife Anna Elisabetha had baptized:
1. Maria Catharina, died 25 July 1707 aged 1 day (appears in burial records)
2. Joh. Jerg, born 1 Apr 1709, baptized 5 Apr 1709—died 2 Jan 1710
3. Joh. Ludwig, born 16 Dec 1710, baptized 18 Dec 1710—died 5 (?) May 1713
4. Margaretha, born 26 Feb 1716, baptized 27 Feb 1716—died 30 Sep 1718
5. Anna Barbara, born Feb/Mar 1718 (birth and baptism obscured)
6. Johann Georg, born 30 Mar 1720, baptized 1 Apr 1720

Married 7 Dec 1728: Christoph Adam Becher, son of Joh. Georg Becher, schoolmaster, and Margaretha, daughter of Sebastian Reinacher (Note: Margaretha's 1762 burial recorded in Russheim records.)

Died 5 Jan 1766: Christoph Adam Becher, citizen, aged 68 years, 9 months, 4 ½ days

Died 15 (18?) April 1732: Johann Georg Becher, aged 64 (84?) years, 10 months, and 15 days. [I cannot read the German of the full entry—"35 years and 2 months" appears, which may be the time that he served as the village's schoolmaster.]

IMMIGRATION SEARCH:

Hacker, *Auswanderung aus Baden und dem Breisgau*:

Hacker Emigrant 467:
Elisabeth Becher, widow, of Russheim. 1737. Destination not stated. (Johann Haushalter and Martin Jock applied at the same time—both were rejected. It is assumed Elisabeth Becher would have traveled with them. The two men did emigrate successfully in 1739 and arrived at Philadelphia that year.)

Clifford Neal Smith, *Emigrants from the West-German Fuerstenberg Territories.*

Elisabeth Becher, widow, Russheim, 1737 to America. Planned to accompany Johann Hausshalter and Martin Joeck.

Ship *Friendship*, qualified 20 Sep 1738 at Philadelphia:

Valentin Schaller, age 24
Michel Karcher, age 46
<u>Hans Jörg Becher, age 18</u>
Johannes Kuhn, age 30
Debalt Klingler, age 24

AMERICAN COLONIAL RECORDS:

There were a number of men named George Becher in early Pennsylvania records; however, I could find no person of this name connected to known Russheimers.

Christina Boltz

In 1752, Russheim widow Christina Boltz went to America with her daughter Maria Margaretha, aged 14 years. Presumably, to undertake such a long and dangerous trip, they traveled with a larger group. All known Russheim emigrants of 1752 who went to America traveled on the Ship *Rawley*.

According to Werner Hacker's research, the <u>widow</u> Christina Boltz was manumitted with her daughter Margaretha in 1752. In the Russheim records, I found two married women named Christina Boltz who had children circa 1735 to 1745. One—the late wife of Adam Boltz—married in 1750 as a widow to Johann Michael Weber. That Christina did not have a daughter named Margaretha baptized in the Russheim records.

I believe the other Christina—delineated below—to be the emigrant. However, if it were she, then she left her 18-year-old son Philipp in Russheim.

GERMAN RECORDS:

Spöck Evangelisch KB:

Hans Georg Rüger & his wife Catharina Barbara had baptized:
1. Eva Christina, born 22 Aug 1715, baptized 24 Aug 1715
2. Rosina Margaretha, born 1 Nov 1717

Above: 1715 baptism of Eva Christina Ruger in the Spock Evangelisch records. Landeskirchliches Archiv Karlsruhe > Spöck > Mischbuch 1667 - 1729 - Bild 116 (Accessed via Archion.de)

Russheim Evangelisch KB:

Married 11 Nov 1732: Johann Georg Boltz, son of Wendel Boltz, and Eva Christina, daughter of Joh. Georg Rüger of Spöck

Georg Boltz & his wife Christina, born Rügerin, had baptized:
1. Joh. Philipp, born 31 Oct 1733 –died 1 Mar 1808
2. Margaretha, born 27 Sep 1737, baptized 28 Sep 1737

Died 28 June 1738: Georg Boltz, aged 54 years

IMMIGRATION:

Hacker, *Auswanderungen aus Baden und dem Breisgau.*

Emigrant 957: Christina Boltz, widow, of Russheim, 1752 to America with her daughter Maria Margaretha, age 14

PENNSYLVANIA RECORDS:

Several persons named Boltz resided in what is now Lebanon County, Pennsylvania, in the 1740s and 1750s. One of them—Michael Boltz—emigrated from nearby Eggenstein.

Georg Braun (and possibly his brother Adam Braun)

1752 Rawley

They came in groups.

Georg Braun appears on the passenger list of the Ship *Rawley* signing next to Johannes Seitz (q.v.). In Russheim, Georg Braun had married Johannes' sister Margaretha Seitzin.

Of interest, an Adam Braun appears in Lancaster County, Pennsylvania, records in the same community as Georg Braun and other Russheimers. In 1747, an Adam Braun deserted the village. This deserter is presumably the Adam Braun, brother to Georg Braun.

GERMAN RECORDS:

Russheim Evangelisch KB:

Married 4 Sep 1708: Hans Braun, widower, married Anna Catharina, legitimate daughter of Johan Georg Oberlin of Liedolsheim

Johann Braun & his wife Anna Catharina had baptized:
1. Anna Catharina, born 12 May 1710, baptized 13 May 1710—died 1790
2. Maria Barbara, born 27 Oct 1712, baptized 28 Oct 1712
3. Johann Martin, born 1 Aug 1715, baptized 2 Aug 1715
4. Joh. Georg, born 1 Jan 1717, baptized 2 Jan 1717
5. Maria Catharina, born 15 July 1718, baptized 16 July 1718
6. Johann Adam, born 14 Jan 1722, baptized 15 Jan 1722

Died 26 Jan 1745: Johannes Braun, born at Liedolsheim, aged 77 years

Above: 1717 baptism of Joh. Georg Braun. Landeskirchliches Archiv Karlsruhe > Rußheim > Mischbuch 1692 - 1738 - Bild 34 (Accessed via Archion.de)

Married --- 1740: Georg Braun and Margaretha Seitzin, daughter of Martin Seitz (extremely difficult to read on darkened microfilm image)

Johann Georg Braun & his wife Margaretha, born Seitzin, had baptized:
1. Margaretha, born 24 Jan 1741
2. Johann Georg, baptized 11 Sep 1743—died 11 Sep 1749
3. Christina (twin), born 15 Mar 1746, baptized 15 Mar 1746—died 26 Mar 1746 (date of death difficult to read)
4. Anna Catharina (twin), born 15 Mar 1746, baptized 15 Mar 1746—died 9 Oct 1749

IMMIGRATION:

Hacker, *Auswanderung aus Baden und dem Breisgau:*

Hacker Emigrant 1065:
Adam Braun, Russheim, deserted the village, May 1747.

Hacker Emigrant 1072:
Joh. Georg Braun, Russheim, with wife and one child, "überschuldet" (fault). Manumitted 7 Mar 1752.

Ship *Rawley*, qualified 23 Oct 1752 at Philadelphia:

Hans Jerg Steidinger
Johan Philip (X) Frech
George (X) Brown
Johannes Seitz
Lorentz (X) Houshalter
Joseph Burgstahler
Christoph Hacker
Michel Lang

PENNSYLVANIA RECORDS:

For consideration only:

Warwick Lutheran KB, Lancaster County, Pennsylvania:

Georg Braun had baptized:
1. Johann Georg, born 1 Sep 1754, baptized 16 Sep 1754, sp. George Wehre & Catharina Lauberin

Adam Braun & his wife Lisabetha sponsored child of Friederich Wilhelm Hagger on 20 Sep 1761

Cocalico Township, Lancaster County, Tax Records (1751-1789):

George Braun, laborer, 1756-1759. inmate

Georg Ulrich Britz

1749

Not every hopeful journey ended as planned. Georg Ulrich Britz died during passage, leaving a widow and children to find their way in the New Land.

GERMAN RECORDS:

Russheim Evangelisch KB:

Veit Werner & his wife Margaretha had baptized:
1. Maria Margaretha, baptized 18 Mar 1708
2. Veitus, born 15 Apr 1712, baptized 16 Apr 1712
3. Johann Michael, born 29 Oct 1714, baptized 30 Oct 1714
4. Anna Barbara, born 28 Mar 1717, baptized 28 Mar 1717
5. Anna Catharina Werner born 3 Jan 1719, baptized 4 Jan 1719

Married 10 May 1740: Georg Ulrich Britz and Anna Catharina Werner, daughter of Veit Werner. They had baptized:
1. Johann Adam, born 24 Jan 1741
2. Johann Georg, born 8 Aug 1742
3. Christoph, born 29 Apr 1744

Note: In regards to the marriage record, the microfilm image is dark and difficult to read. There appears to be other information of value in regards to the groom. He does not appear to be from Russheim.

IMMIGRATION:

Hacker, *Auswanderung aus Baden und dem Breisgau:*

Hacker Emigrant 1159:
Ulrich Britz, Russheim, *schleifmuhlenbestander*, with wife and five children to Pennsylvania, manumitted 24 Apr 1749.

Ulrich Britz has not been located in the 1749 passenger lists of arrivals at Philadelphia. He presumably would have been aboard the same ship as the other 1749 Russheim emigrants.

Those emigrant families—Hacker, Mock, Elser, Keller, Neess—all arrived on the Ship Ann and qualified 28 Sep 1749 at Philadelphia.

Ulrich's presumed widow Catharina married Casper Bickins on January 19, 1750 at St. Michael's Lutheran church in Philadelphia. No estate records for Ulrich Britz were found in Philadelphia County.

Ulrich likely died during the passage from Russheim to Philadelphia.

PENNSYLVANIA RECORDS:

St. Michael's Lutheran KB, Philadelphia, Philadelphia County, Pennsylvania:

Married 19 Jan 1750: Casper Bickins, widower, and Catharina Britz, widow

For further consideration:

A George Britz & wife Margaretha had children baptized in York County from 1766 to 1770.

A Johann Adam Britz married Margaret Stover and resided in Cumberland County before moving to Botetourt County, Virginia, where he died in 1832. This family's surname evolved to Britts.

Joseph Burgstahler

1752 Rawley

Joseph Burgstahler arrived at Philadelphia aboard the Ship *Rawley* in 1752. This man signed his name in the midst of six emigrants from Russheim. I believe this American immigrant to be the Joseph Burgstahler of Russheim, son of Joseph Burgstahler, the elder.

I have found no record of Joseph Burgstahler in Colonial records after arrival at Philadelphia. However, a few scattered records pertaining to Burgstahler females can be found in Berks County, Pennsylvania, records. The names fit the daughters of Adam Burgstahler of Spöck, a German village near Russheim. Adam Burgstahler and Joseph Burgstahler, the elder, were brothers. Adam was manumitted in 1739, but his intended destination was not given. I speculate that Adam emigrated to America. If true, then it is likely that Joseph Burgstahler of Russheim would have tried to locate near to Adam's heirs in the American colonies.

GERMAN RECORDS:

Spöck Evangelisch KB:

Married 26 Oct 1697: Simon Burgstahler, son of Benedict Burgstahler, and Anna Catharina, daughter of Georg Nagel.

Simon Burgstahler & his wife Anna Catharina had baptized:
1. Hans Simon, born 26 Oct 1698, baptized 28 Oct 1698—died 26 Aug 1759
2. Johann Martin, born 12 Feb 1701, baptized 13 Feb 1701—died 29 July 1701
3. Johann Adam, born 26 Feb 1703, baptized 28 Feb 1703
4. Joseph, born 18 Feb 1706, baptized 19 Feb 1706
5. Anna Catharina, born 24 Aug 1707, baptized 25 Aug 1707—died 19 Feb 1717
6. Anna Eva, born 18 Mar 1710, baptized 19 Mar 1710
7. Anna Barbara, born 6 July 1712

Married 1724: Johann Adam Burgstahler and Catharina Barbara Straussin.

Hans Adam Burgstahler & his wife Catharina Barbara had baptized:
1. Johann Adam, born 15 Jan 1725, baptized 16 Jan 1725
2. Johann Georg, born 17 Aug 1726--died 7 Aug 1729
3. Anna Catharina, born 28 Feb 1728
4. Christoph, born 15 Mar 1730, baptized 16 Mar 1730—died 23 Mar 1731

Died 24 Feb 1731: Catharina Barbara Burgstahler, wife of Adam Burgstahler, aged 25 years

Married 20 Nov 1731: Johann Adam Burgstahler, widower, and Anna Catharina, daughter of Johann Martin Nagel.

5. Eva Christina, born 17 Oct 1732, baptized 18 Oct 1732
6. Maria Margaretha, born 18 Dec 1735, baptized 20 Dec 1735
7. Maria Magdalena, baptized 22 Feb 1739

Russheim Evangelisch KB:

Married 6 May 1732: Joseph Burgstaller, son of Simon Burgstaller of Spock, married Elisabetha, daughter of Daniel Müller

Joseph Burgstahler & his wife Elisabetha, born Müllerin, had baptized:
1. Johannes, born 5 Jan 1733—died 1736
2. Joseph, born 10 July 1734, baptized 11 July 1734
3. Joh. Peter, born 22 Dec 1736, baptized 23 Dec 1736—died 29 July 1760
4. Stillborn child, born 29 Mar 1740

Died 6 Apr 1740: Elisabetha, wife of Joseph Burgstahler, born Müllerin, aged 30 years and 4 days

Married 25 Jan 1745: Joseph Burgstahler, widower, and Rosina Weberin, widow.

Joseph Burgstahler & his wife Rosina Hornerin had baptized:
1. Christina, born 4 July 1747, baptized 4 July 1747

Died 27 Dec 1748: Joseph Burgstahler, citizen and smith, aged 44 years

IMMIGRATION:

Hacker, *Auswanderung aus Baden und dem Breisgau:*

Hacker Emigrant 1281:
Joh. Adam Burgstahler of Spöck, manumitted 11 Aug 1739, destination unknown.

Not found in Strassburger and Hinke. See the Pennsylvania church records abstracted below. The Burgstahler girls who appear in records circa 1748 to 1755 fit the profile of Adam Burgstahler's daughters from Spöck.

A Joseph Burgstahler arrived at Philadelphia aboard the Ship Rawley in 1752. This man signed his name in the midst of six emigrants from Russheim. I believe him to be the Joseph Burgstahler born in Russheim Anno 1734.

Ship *Rawley*, qualified 23 Oct 1752 at Philadelphia:

Hans Jerg Steidinger
Johan Philip (X) Frech
George (X) Brown
Johannes Seitz
Lorentz (X) Houshalter
Joseph Burgstahler
Christoph Hacker
Michel Lang
Matheas (X) Miller

Hans Jorg Mock
Hans Jorg Wächter
--All signed next to each other.

PENNSYLVANIA RECORDS:

I did not locate in Colonial Records after arrival at Philadelphia.

Another Burgstahler family arrived prior to Joseph Burgstahler. Due to the rarity of this surname, records are given below. Descendants claim that Margaretha Burgstaller, wife of George Dice (or Deiss), later removed to Pendleton County, Virginia (now West Virginia).

Christ Lutheran KB, Stouchsburg, Berks County, Pennsylvania:

Confirmed 21 Apr 1745: Eva Christina Burgstahl
Confirmed 14 May 1749: Maria Margre. Burckstaller

Peter Muller & Christina Burchstaler sponsored child of Wendel & Anna Maria Müller on 3 Sep 1749
Joh. Adam Fischer and Christina Burchstoler sponsored child of Joh. Peter & Elis. Margaretha Wagner on 17 Sep 1749

Joh. Georg Class and Margretha Burckstahler sponsored child of Jacob & A. Maria Seltzer on 1 Dec 1754

Host KB, Berks County, Pennsylvania:

George Dice married 7 Sep 1755 Margaretha Burgstaller

Elser (or Eltzer) Family

1749 Ann

This migrant family's origins were documented long ago in a paper entitled "The Elser Homestead and Family History" (*Historical Papers and Addresses of the Lancaster County Historical Society*, Volume 15, page 52). The findings in the Russheim records both add to and correct facts in that paper.

GERMAN RECORDS:

Russheim Evangelisch KB:

Paulus Speck & his wife Catharina Schmidt had baptized:
   1. Maria Barbara, born 10 Feb 1699

Married 9 May 1719: Hans Adam Eltzer, son of Conrad Eltzer and Maria Barbara Spöck, daughter of Johann Paulus Spöck

Johann Adam Elzer & his wife Maria Barbara had baptized:
   1. Joh. Georg, born 21 Jan 1720, baptized 23 Jan 1720—died 21 May 1726
   2. Anna Catharina, born 9 Jan 1722, baptized 11 Jan 1722

Died 15 July 1725: Maria Barbara, wife of Hans Adam Elser, aged 26 years

----

Married 9 Dec 1726: Hans Adam Elsser, widower, and Margaretha Hagerin

Johann Adam Elsser & his wife Margaretha, born Hagerin, had baptized:
   1. Johann Adam, born 17 Aug 1727, baptized 31 Aug 1727
   2. Maria Barbara, born 19 July 1728—died 3 Aug 1728
   3. Christina, born 13 July 1729
   4. Peter, born 21 June 1731 (month difficult to read) [cross next to name?]
   5. Maria Barbara, born 17 Oct 1732, baptized 19 Oct 1732 (cross next to name?)
   6. Johannes, born 22 Apr 1734, baptized 23 Apr 1734---died 16 Mar 1737
   7. Eva, born 9 May 1739, baptized 11 May 1739

Died 17 July 1740: Adam Elser, son of Conrad Elser & Anna Barbara, nee Boltzin, aged 51 years

Landeskirchliches Archiv Karlsruhe > Rußheim > Mischbuch 1738 - 1777,Apr. 1800,1817 - Bild 108

Important: American records suggest that Adam & Margaretha Elser's children Peter and Mara Barbara lived in Pennsylvania. However, next to the name of each child in the Russheim baptismal register, the pastor appears to have written a cross—generally indicating that the child had died.

But--I did not locate a burial record for either child in Russheim records. Perhaps the notation was intended for another purpose (e.g., departed). I did closely read baptismal records from 1734 to 1741 to see if another child of that name was born to this couple.

Above: The mark written below Peter Elser's name (baptized 1731) in the Russheim register.

Married 17 Apr 1749: Heinrich Mock, son of ??? (Adam?), from Graben (?) married Margaretha Elserin, widow of Adam

Landeskirchliches Archiv Karlsruhe > Rußheim > Mischbuch 1738 - 1777, Apr. 1800, 1817 - Bild 239

I had great difficulty reading the marriage record above. It would seem of great interest to descendants. The source below suggests the gist of the words the pastor wrote:

> From *In Search of Peace and Prosperity: New German Settlements in Eighteenth-Century Europe and America,* edited by Hartmut Lehmann and Hermann Wellenreuther. Penn State Press, 2010, page 160:
>
> "As in the case of Margaretha Elser and Barbara Schmid, two widows from Russheim, illustrates, the obligations of prospective migrants might even become a public affair. Both widows planned to marry men from outside the village, both fiancés had been denied permission to take up residence in

Russheim, and both widows thereafter decided to emigrate to Pennsylvania. ... [T]he village pastor could speak only of a 'desperate resolution' the two women had taken."

Adam & Margaretha Elser's daughter Catharina remained in Russheim:

Married 5 Dec 1741: Johann Adam Schmidt, son of Adam Schmidt, and Anna Catharina Elser, Johann Adam Elser's daughter. They had baptized:
1. Anna Catharina, baptized 7 Dec 1743, sp. Barbara, wife of Michael Schmidt
2. Christina, baptized 22 Oct 1745—died 1 Apr 1823
3. Johann Adam, baptized 25 Oct 1747 (cross next to child's name)

--Other children not pursued..

IMMIGRATION:

Hacker, *Auswanderung aus Baden und dem Breisgau:*

Hacker Emigrant 1874:
Margarete Elser, widow, of Russheim, born Hager, will go to Pennsylvania *mit mdrjährigen Sohn "Mock" aus Graben. Darf veräussern, wenn Kds-Vm im Land deponiert bleibt.* Manumitted 17 Apr 1749.

Hacker Emigrant 3384:
Margarete Hager, widow of Elsser, of Russheim, with her children. She will marry a son of *des Htrs Mock* of Graben (*wo sie nicht eingelassen wird*). Dated 1 February 1749. (She intends to marry a man surnamed Mock of Graben who will not be accepted into the village.)

Ship *Ann*, qualified 28 Sep 1749 at Philadelphia:

Adam Schaulling
Daniel Scheübly
<u>Henrich Mock</u>
<u>Petter Elser</u>
<u>Hans Adam Hacker</u>
Johann Jacob (X) Sutz
Michel Hengsd [sic]

PENNSYLVANIA RECORDS:

From *Historical Papers and Addresses of the Lancaster County Historical Society*, Volume 15, page 52, "The Elser Homestead and Family History":

"We learn from existing documents of an agreement, or contract, of one Henrich Mock, of Warwick township, Lancaster county, and his wife, which sets forth that he (Mock) agrees to accept and provide for her children left under care by her late husband, Hans Adam Elser as his own. The children mentioned are Christina, Peter, Barbara, and Eve. This document is dated April 28, 1753."

Note: The writers of this 1911 article were unaware that Henrich Mock and Margaretha Elser had married in Germany. They also were unaware of Adam Elser's first marriage.

Warwick Lutheran KB, Lancaster County, Pennsylvania:

(complete for Mock and Elser to 1798 with the exception of communicant records)

Heinrich Mock & his wife Margaretha sponsored child of Georg Stober & his wife Eva on 8 Sep 1759

Peter Elsser & Margaretha Högie sponsored child of Jacob Walter on 5 Mar 1754

Peter Elser had baptized:

1. Georg, born 12 Feb 1765, baptized Estomihi 1765, sp. Georg Michael Eichelberger & his wife

Peter Elzer & his wife Margaretha sponsored child of Georg Stober on 14 Mar 1771

Georg Michael Eichelberger had baptized:
1. Maria Barbara, born 20 Aug 1760, baptized 21 Aug 1760, sp. Heinrich Mock and & his wife Margaretha
2. Magdalena, born 21 Aug 1763, baptized 14 Trinity 1763, sp. Peter Elser & his wife
3. Christina, born 18 Dec 1766, baptized 4 Advent 1766, sp. Peter Elser & his wife

Peter Elser & his wife Catharina had baptized:
1. Georg, born 22 Dec 1787, baptized 4 May 1788, sp. Georg Elzer
2. Elisabeth, born 21 June 1789, baptized 23 Aug 1789, sp. Ludwig Wolfarth & his wife Margreth
3. Johannes, born 12 Mar 1791, baptized 1 May 1791, sp. Joh. Wächter & his wife Elisabeth
4. Petrus, born 14 Dec 1792, baptized 20 May 1793, sp. Johannes Wächter & his wife Elisabeth

Peter Elser & his wife Catharina sponsored child of Johannes Waechter & his wife Elisabeth on 28 May 1792

Peter Elser & his wife Elisabeth had baptized:
1. Catharina, born 6 Aug 1795, baptized 8 Nov 1795, sp. Georg Hacker & Catharina Wächter
2. Margreth, born 20 Oct 1797, baptized 3 Dec 1797, sp. Friderich Wachter & Margreth Elzerin

Peter Elser & his wife Elizabeth sponsored child of Jacob Weiman & his wife Elizabeth on 9 May 1798

Confirmed 1780 Trinity I:
Adam Elzer
Georg Elzer
Peter Elzer

Georg Mock married 21 Apr 1761 Sophia Millerin

Georg Mock had baptized:
1. Catharina, born 10 Sep 1762, baptized 31 Oct 1762, sp. Henrich Mok and Catharina Mullerin
2. Daniel, born 8 Dec 1763, baptized Palmarum 1764, sp. Christoph Oberlin and Catharina Mullerin
3. Christoph, born 30 Jan 1766, baptized 22 June 1766, sp. Christoph Oberlin and Catharina Millerin
4. Christina, born 26 Jan 1769, baptized 11 Apr 1769, sp. Jacob Müller & his wife Anna Maria
5. Georg, born 5 June 1771, baptized 22 June 1771, sp. Jacob Müller & his wife Anna Maria

Georg Mock & his wife Sophia sponsored child of Jacob Müller on 10 Mar 1771
Georg Mock & his wife Sophia sponsored child of Joseph Binkly & his wife Barbara on 19 Apr 1772

Stoever, Rev. John Casper, personal register:

Married 25 Nov 1754: Christina Elser and George Michael Eichelberger (Warwick congregation)
Married 6 Nov 1758: Eva Elszer and George Stober (Warwick congregation)
Married 16 Nov 1760: Peter Elsser and Anna Margaretha Stoever (Warwick congregation)

Peter Elszer & his wife Anna Margaretha of the Warwick congregation had baptized:
1. Peter, born 14 Feb 1767, baptized 23 Mar 1767, sp. George Michael Eichelberger & his wife

Catharina Barbara Gangwolff

A Catharina Barbara Gangwolff was manumitted from the village in 1749. She had apparently departed at least on year prior. She was the daughter of the late mayor of the village. Her mother and siblings remained in the village. There is no evidence of marriage—and I see no evidence that she departed with other Russheimers. Unusual, to say the list.

In the section on the Braun (q.v.) family, I noted that an Adam Braun deserted the village in 1747. He is the only other person who seems to have left the village—at least so far as emigration records indicate—at the same time.

GERMAN RECORDS:

Russheim Evangelisch KB:

Married 26 Oct 1706: Michael, son of Hans Diebold Gangwolfen, and Anna Margaretha, daughter of Peter Giegel

Joh. Michael Gangwolf and his wife Anna Margaretha had baptized:
1. Joh. Michael, born 18 Aug 1707
2. Joh. Jacob, born 17 Apr 1711, baptized 19 Apr 1711
3. Anna Catharina, born 15 May 1713
4. Johannes Casparus, born 30 Dec 1714, baptized 31 Dec 1714—died 22 Dec 1794
5. Johann Michael, born 28 Apr 1717, baptized 20 Apr 1717 (cross next to child's name)
6. Catharina Barbara, born 23 Jan 1719, baptized 23 Jan 1719
7. Maria Barbara, born 6 Jan 1722, baptized 8Jan 1722—died 13.10.1778
8. Johannes, born 3 Mar 1724, baptized 4 Mar 1724
9. Maria Christina, born 26 May 1726, baptized 28 May 1726—died 21 Nov 1786

Died 4 Mar 1739: Johann Michael Gangwolff, Schultheissen, aged 66 years

Died 18 Apr 1753: Anna Margaretha, widow of Joh. Michael Gangwolfin, burger and schultheissin, aged 66 years

----

Married 21 Jan 1738: Joh. Casper Gangwolff, son of Hans M. Gangwolfin, schultheissen, and Anna Catharina, daughter of Jacob Schmidt of this place. They had baptized:
1. A daughter, born 16 Jan 1741. (The child has no name and there are no sponsors. Apparently the child was born dead.)

Married 4 Dec 1739: Joh. Michael Schmidt, son of Georg Schmidt, and Maria Barbara Gangwolf, daughter of Michael Gangwolf, schultheissen

Married 17 Nov 1744: Johann Friedrich Reinacher, smith, son of Johann Georg Reinacher, and Maria Christina Gangwolfin, daughter of Johann Michael Gangwolff, schultheissen (village headsman)

Married ---1745 (date obscured on microfilm): Johann Casper Gangwolf, widower, and Catharina Barbara Haasin, daughter of Johann Adam Haasin

Died 25 Apr 1743: Anna Catharina Gangwolfin, born Schmidtin, the wife of Johann Casper Gangwolffin. She was born 8 Feb 1717. She married Casper Gangwolffin on 21 Jan 1738.

Johann Casper Gangwolf and his wife Catharina Barbara Haasin had baptized:
1. Joh. Adam, born 26 Oct 1746, baptized 26 Oct 1746—died 27 Oct 1746
2. Johannes, born 30 June 1748, baptized the same day—died 29 Aug 1824
3. Christina, born 21 Aug 1751
4. Maria Barbara, born 30 Nov 1753, baptized 2 Dec 1753—died 17 May 1824
5. Catharina Barbara, born 3 July 1756

--Not pursued further. Catharina Barbara Gangwolffin, wife of Johann Casper Gangwolff, could not be the emigrant to Pennsylvania.

IMMIGRATION:

Hacker, *Auswanderung aus Baden und dem Breisgau:*

Hacker Emigrant 2614:
Catharina Barbara Gangwolff, Russheim/deceased (?), Michael (I am uncertain of Hacker's notations. A cross appears a forwards slash. The Michael Gangwolff, schultheissen, of Russheim—father of Catharina Barbara Gangwolff—died in 1753.

"vor 1 Jahr nach Pennsylvania": In Pennsylvania for one year.

"Lässt durch Mutter um Manumission bitten" (roughly, "please let through the mother")

"Mutter vw Schultheissin Gangwolf": Her mother is the wife of the village headsman Gangwolff.

"weist vermögen nach, zahlt manumission": roughly, has riches, pays manumission

Joachim Siedel, German researcher, translation:

> "One year before March 1749, Catharina Barbara Gangwolff, daughter of the late Joh. Michael Gangwolff, former headsman of Russheim village, left her home for Pennsylvania. As this required the payment of a local manumission, Catharina Barbara, as an unmarried woman not being contractually capable herself, let her widowed mother give proof to the authorities about her assets and pay the manumission for her. Whether Catharina Barbara had emigrated alone, or whether she had married shortly before, is currently uncertain."

PENNSYLVANIA RECORDS:

I was unable to locate evidence of this emigrant in American records. For consideration: Adam Braun deserted the village of Russheim in 1747. Did he depart with the Catharina Barbara Gangwolff?

Christoph Hacker & sons Hans Adam Hacker and Johann Georg Hacker

Christoph Hacker of Russheim and his four children migrated to Pennsylvania over a period of three years. Only the father appears in German emigration records. Sons Adam (1749) and Georg (1751) departed first. In 1752, father Christoph and daughters Christina, wife of Michael Lang (q.v.), and Margaretha, wife of Lorentz Haushalter (q.v.), arrived at Philadelphia on the Ship *Rawley* with other Russheimers.

The Hacker family settled in Cocalico Township, Lancaster County, near to other Russheim emigrants (son Georg would later move to Philadelphia). The surname evolved to Hocker. Family genealogist Kris Hocker has done extensive research on this family. Please visit www.krishocker.com for more extensive information.

GERMAN RECORDS:

Russheim Evangelisch Records:

Hans Stephan Hacker & his wife Anna Maria had baptized:
 1. Christoph, born 2 May 1697

Christoph Hacker, son of Hans Stephan Hacker, married 9 Feb 1722 Anna Margaretha Jock. They had baptized:
 1. Christina, born 25 Dec 1723
 2. Maria Catharina, born 4 Sep 1725—died 21 Nov 1726
 3. Johann Adam, born 28 Oct 1727
 4. Anna Margaretha, born 24 Dec 1730
 5. Johann Georg, born 4 Apr 1734

Married 8 Nov 1746: Johann Micheal Lang and Christina Hacker. (Note: I am taking this date from other researchers. On the microfilm record available to me, the marriages near this date are too darkened to read. I can make out "Michael.")

Joh. Michael Lang and his wife Christina, nee Hacker, had baptized:
 1. Johann Georg, born 6 Nov 1747, baptized 6 Nov 1747
 2. Christina, born 18 Dec 1751, baptized 18 Dec 1751 (Pastor's notation: "went to the new land")

Married 24 Nov 1750: Lorenz Haushalter, son of Lorentz Haushalter, and Anna Margaretha, daughter of Christoph Hacker.

Lorentz Haushalter & his wife Margaretha, born Hackerin, had baptized:
 1. Johann Georg, born 29 Nov 1751, baptized 1 Dec 1751. Pastor's notations: "zog ist neue Land."

IMMIGRATION:

Hacker, *Auswanderung aus Baden und dem Breisgau:*

Hacker Emigrant 3405:
Christof Hacker, *schuster*, of Russheim. Manumitted April 1752.

Ship *Ann*, qualified 28 Sep 1749 at Philadelphia:

Adam Schaulling
Daniel Scheübly
Henrich Mock
Petter Elser
Hans Adam Hacker
Johann Jacob (X) Sutz

Ship *Brothers*, qualified 16 Sep 1751 at Philadelphia:

Christof Weber
Georg Hacker
Peter Abert (sic: Albert?)
Johannes Schmitt

Ship *Rawley*, qualified 23 Oct 1752 at Philadelphia:

Johan Philip (X) Frech
George (X) Brown
Johannes Seitz
Lorentz (X) Houshalter
Joseph Burgstahler
Christoph Hacker
Michel Lang
Matheas (X) Miller
Hans Jorg Mock
--All signed next to each other.

PENNSYLVANIA RECORDS:

Warwick Lutheran KB, Elizabeth Township, Lancaster County, Pennsylvania:

Johann Georg Haker had baptized:
1. Georg, born 22 Oct 1756, baptized [not given], sp. Georg Wittman & his wife
2. Johannes, born 11 Jan 1760, baptized [not given], sp. Georg Wittman & his wife
3. Martin, born 10 Feb 1762, baptized [not given], sp. George Wächter and Catharina Weidmennin

George Hakker and Margaretha Weidmennin sponsored child of Laurenty Haushalter on 28 Jul 1754

Johann Adam Hacker had baptized:
1. Fridrich, born 17 Jan 1756, baptized [not given], sp. Wendel Weidmann & his wife
2. Johannes, born 27 Jan 1758, baptized [not given], sp. Jacob Baker and Barbara Widmennin
3. Christoph, born 21 Feb 1760, baptized [not given], sp. Christoph Weidmann
4. Christina, born 19 Apr 1762, baptized [not given], sp. Bernard Gertner & his wife
5. Johann Adam, born 20 Feb 1764, baptized [not given], sp., sp. Bernard Gertner & his wife
6. Johann Georg, born 9 Oct 1766, baptized 12 Oct 1766, sp. Lorenz Haushalter & his wife
7. Martin, born 21 Oct 1768, baptized 29 Nov 1768, sp. Lorentz Haushalter
8. Catharina, born 21 Jan 1771, baptized 27 Jan 1771, sp. Lorentz Haushalter & his wife
9. Elisabeth, born 23 Feb 1773, baptized 21 Mar 1773, sp. Lorentz Haushalter & his wife Margaretha

Adam Haker & his wife Elisabetha sponsored child of Christoph Weidmann on 16 Dec 1753

Joh. Adam Haker sponsored child of Laurently Haushalter on 21 Feb 1766

Adam Haker (or Hacker) & his wife Elisabeth sponsored child of Lorentz Haushalter on 13 Jan 1768 and 20 Jul 1770 and 19 Apr 1772 and 18 Sep 1774

Adam Hacker & his wife Elisabetha sponsored child of Christian Stäbler on 19 Nov 1760

Lancaster County, Pennsylvania, Orphans Court Records:

Estate of Adam Hacker, late of Cocalico Township.
1. Proceedings dated 4 Mar 1783: Petition of eldest son Frederick Hacker and second son John Hacker: That their father Adam Hacker lately died intestate seized in possession of two tracts of land: (1.) 212A Cocalico Township, patented land; and (2.) 7A Cocalico Township, warranted land. That their said father left a widow and nine children, five of whom are yet minors. –The court orders the land to be valued and appraised by 12 disinterested persons by the next General Orphans Court.
2. Proceedings dated 3 June 1783: After reviewing the report, the court confirms both aforesaid properties unto eldest son Frederick Hacker, subject to paying the other heirs their due shares out of the valation. The deceased left a widow named Elizabeth and issue the following children: Frederick Hacker, John Hacker, Christopher Hacker, Christina (the wife of Henry Fetter), Adam Hacker, George Hacker, Martin Hacker, Elizabeth Hacker, and Jacob Hacker.

Johann Adam Haushalter and siblings

1739 Friendship

Johannes Haushalter of Russheim married twice and had issue six children who lived to maturity. Circumstantial evidence suggests that four of these children went to America. The father Johannes may also have departed, as there is no further record of him in the church register after 1739.

In 1739, Martin Jock (q.v.) and Johann Adam Haushalter arrived at Philadelphia aboard the Ship *Friendship*. This Adam Haushalter was the son of the said Johannes Haushalter. In 1725 his father had married Maria Elisabeth, daughter of Georg Jock, as his second wife. Maria Elisabeth and the aforesaid Martin Jock were brother and sister.

Perhaps Johannes Haushalter departed Russheim but died during passage. (No other person surname Haushalter is on the 1739 Friendship passenger list, which legally had to include all males aged 16 years and upwards.) Pennsylvania records suggest that four of his children married in Lancaster County, Pennsylvania, from 1741 to 1746 (see Pastor Stoever's records below). In 1742, Pastor Stoever also recorded the marriage of Joseph Obold and Elisabeth Haushalter. This Elisabeth Haushalter cannot be placed as a child of Johannes Haushalter. Might she have been a Johannes Haushalter's widow? Pastor Stoever did not typically identify widows and widowers in his marriage records. Joseph Obold died in Bern Township, Berks County, in 1770. His estate records give no indication of stepchildren.

Brothers Johann Adam Haushalter and Johann Georg Haushalter left a remarkable trail of records.

GERMAN RECORDS:

Russheim Evangelisch KB:

Johannes Haushalter married 7 Nov 1713 Anna Maria Barbara Siegel. They had baptized:
1. Johann Michael, born 21 Feb 1715—died 15 July 1782 (date of death added later by pastor)
2. Johannes, born 18 Oct 1716
3. Maria Margaretha, born 28 June 1718
4. Hans Adam, born 20 Dec 1719
5. Maria Barbara, born 25 Sep 1721
6. Johann Georg, born 13 Aug 1723—died 23 Oct 1723 (cross next to name in baptismal register)

Anna Barbara Haushalter died 26 Mar 1725.

Married 27 Nov 1725: Johannes Haushalter, widower (wittwer), and Maria Elisabetha, daughter of Georg Jock. They had baptized:
1. Johann Georg, baptized 20 June 1727

IMMIGRATION:

Hacker, *Auswanderung aus Baden und dem Breisgau*:

Hacker Emigrant 3774:
Haushalter, Johann, Russheim. Application to emigrate rejected. October 1737.

Hacker Emigrant 3775:
Johann Haushalter, Russheim, Intends to go to America. Manumitted 8 Aug 1739. (Note: To arrive at Philadelphia on the Ship *Friendship* in September 1739, this Johan Haushalter would have needed to leave Russheim before this date.)

Ship *Friendship*, qualified 3 Sep 1739 at Philadelphia:

Martin (O) Yoak, age 31
John Philip (+) Herberger
Johan Adam ([) Housholter, age 20
Johan Nicolaus Maurer, age 23 (signed his name)
--*Signed next to each other.*

PENNSYLVANIA RECORDS:

Stoever, Rev. John Casper, personal register:

Married 11 Jul 1741: Johannes Weidman and Margaretha Hausshalter (Cocalico)
Married 29 Mar 1742: Joseph Obold and Elisabetha Hausshalter (Cocalico)
Married 17 Oct 1743: Johann Adam Hausshalter and Maria Elisabetha Weidman (Warwick)
Married 1 Jan 1744: Johann George Wittman and Anna Barbara Hausshalter (Warwick)
Married 18 Nov 1746: Johann Georg Hausshalter and Margaretha Balmer (Warwick)

Adam Hausshalter (Cumru congregation) had baptized:
1. Elisabetha Hausshalter, born 19 Jan 1754, baptized 12 Feb 1754, sp. Johannes Lehn & his wife

Note: Pastor Stoever served various Lutheran congregation. The word in parenthesis is the congregation where the sacrament took place.

Warwick Lutheran KB, Lancaster County, Pennsylvania:

Johannes Weidmann married 6 July 1741 Margaretha Hausshalterin

----

Signers of the Warwick Congregation Church Doctrine, 1743:
Johan Adam Haushalter (note: this signature has occasionally been misinterpreted as Johan Peter Haushalter)

Married 17 Oct 1743: Johann Adam Haushalter and Maria Elisabetha Weidmann

Johannes Adam Hausshalter had baptized:
1. Johann Adam, born 1 Nov 1744, baptized 4 Nov 1744, sp. Johann Valentin Stober & his wife
2. Adam, born 16 Sep 1746, baptized 22 Sep 1746, sp. Joh. Hermann Lehn & his wife
3. Maria Barbara, born 16 Mar 1749, baptized 26 Mar 1749, sp. the above and George Michael Balmer, Jr., & his wife
4. Mattheis, born 30 Nov 1751, baptized 1 Dec 1751, sp. Joh. Herman Lehn & his wife

--Note: *Pastor Stoever first wrote "Johann Hausshalter" as the father. He then inserted "Adam" above. When the church records were transcribed and published by Pastor Frederick S. Weiser in 1983, he missed notice of "Adam" and wrote only Johannes Hausshalter as the father (see the Pennsylvania German Society's Sources and Documents Vol. II: Records of Pastoral Acts at Emanuel Lutheran Church).*

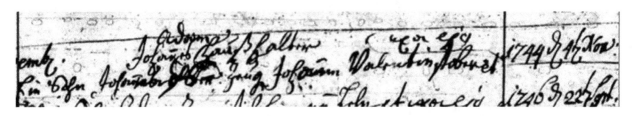

Above: Part of Pastor John Casper Stoever's entry for the family of Johann Adam Haushalter in the Warwick Lutheran church register.. (Source: Historic Pennsylvania Church and Town Records. Philadelphia, Pennsylvania: Historical Society of Pennsylvania. Accessed via Ancestry.com's database Pennsylvania and New Jersey, Church and Town Records, 1669-2013)

Adam Hausshalter & his wife sponsored child of Johannes Weydtmann on 25 Jan 1752

Joh. Georg Hausshalter had baptized:
1. Georg Jacob, born 18 Sep 1747, baptized 20 Sep 1747, sp. Georg Jacob Schnurer & his wife
2. Georg Adam, born 22 Oct 1749, baptized 19 Nov 1749, sp. Georg Michael Balmer & Christina Sussin
3. Georg Michael, born 20 Feb 1753, baptized 4 Mar 1753, sp. Georg Michael Eichelberger & Christina Sussin
4. Catharina Margaretha, born 13 July 1755, baptized 17 Aug 1755, sp. George Michael Balmer & his wife; Emanuel Suss; and Catharina Balmerin
5. Johannes, born 13 July 1758, baptized 18 July 1758, sp. Johannes Weitmann

Joh. Georg Hausshalter & his wife Maria Margaretha and Heinrich Motz & his wife Maria Barbara sponsored child of Georg Jacob Schnurer on 9 Aug 1747

Jerg Hausshalter & his wife sponsored child of Michael Balmer, Jr., on 25 Feb 1759 and [August 1761]

Reading Lutheran KB, Reading, Berks County, Pennsylvania, USA:

(selected only)

Johann Adam Haushalter & his wife Elisabetha had baptized:
1. Maria Margaret, born 15 Dec 1761, baptized Sexagisium 1762, sp. Joh. Nicholas Gauer & his wife Elsiabetha; and the wife of Johannes Lean
2. Catharina, born 19 Jul 1764, baptized 9 Sep 1764, sp. Nicholas Gauer & his wife Elisabetha
3. Anna Maria, born 27 Dec 1765, baptized 14 Feb 1766, sp. Nicholas Gauer & his wife Elisabetha

Johannes Haushalter & his wife Margaretha had baptized:
1. Adam, born 10 Oct 1768, baptized 24 Oct 1768, sp. Adam Haushalter

Washington County, Maryland, Estate Records:

Washington Will A5:
George Householder weaver, of Washington County, writ 20 May 1777, probated 5 Jul 1777.
1. He makes provisions for his wife Margaretha.
2. To my three eldest sons George Jacob, George Adam, and George Michael: My 300-acre tract of land situate in Hamilton Township, Cumberland County, Pennsylvania—to be equally divided among them. (The tract was originally granted by application unto a certain Thomas Freeman, bearing date 27 Mar 1767, No. 3269.)
3. To my six youngest children Margaret, Elizabeth, Catharine, Barbara, John George, and John Householder: The residue of my estate.
4. Executors: My loving brother Johan Adam Householder and my eldest son George Jacob Householder.
5. Signed his name as George Housholter.
6. Witnessed by George Neigh and Michael Househalter.

Washington Will A378:
Adam Householder of Washington County, writ 22 Jul 1791, probated 2 Jan 1798.
1. "being very sick and weak"
2. To my first birth son John Householder: The sum of five pounds.
3. To my children, viz.: John, Adam, Mathias, Barbara, Elisabeth, Christian, Eve, Margaretha, Catharina, and Mary: Equal shares of my estate.
4. Executors: Peter Bussard and Jonathan Moyer.
5. Signed his name with the mark "A."
6. Witnessed by Daniel Bussard, George Hobber, and Jacob Yates.

Lorentz Haushalter

1752 Rawley

Lorentz Haushalter and his wife Margaretha Hacker lived in Warwick Township, Lancaster County, Pennsylvania. In the Warwick Lutheran church records, he and his wife appear frequently together in records with Adam Hacker (q.v.), Margaretha's brother.

GERMAN RECORDS:

Russheim Evangelisch KB:

Lorenz Haushalter & his wife Maria Barbara, nee Hager, had baptized:
1. Johann Georg, born 12 Feb 1723—died 24 Apr 1733
2. Johann Friedrich, born 6 June 1724, baptized 8 June 1724—died 5 Aug 1795
3. Lorenz, baptized 14 Aug 1726
4. Christoph, born 18 Sep 1731—died 7 Jan 1735
5. Anna Catharina, baptized 23 May 1736

Married 24 Nov 1750: Lorentz Haushalter, son of Lorentz Haushalter, and Anna Margaretha, daughter of Christoph Hacker.

Lorentz Haushalter & his wife Margaretha, born Hackerin, had baptized:
1. Johann Georg, born 29 Nov 1751, baptized 1 Dec 1751. Pastor's notations: "zog ist neue Land."

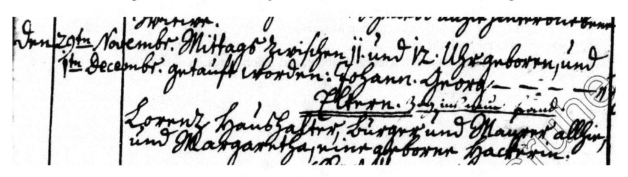

Above: The pastor wrote "went to the new land" (zog im neue land) after the German word Eltern (parents). Landeskirchliches Archiv Karlsruhe > Rußheim > Mischbuch 1738 - 1777, Apr. 1800,1817 - Bild 31 (Accessed via Archion.de)

IMMIGRATION:

Hacker, *Auswanderung aus Baden und dem Breisgau:*

Hacker Emigrant 3653:
Lorenz Hausser, Russheim, with his wife. Manumitted 7 Mar 1752.

Hacker Emigrant 3776:
Lorenz Haushalter, Russheim, with wife. Manumitted 7 Mar 1752. (See emigrant 3653—same person)

Ship *Rawley*, qualified 23 Oct 1752 at Philadelphia:

Hans Jerg Steidinger
Johan Philip (X) Frech
George (X) Brown
Johannes Seitz
Lorentz (X) Houshalter
Joseph Burgstahler
Christoph Hacker
Michel Lang
Matheas (X) Miller
Hans Jorg Mock
Hans Jorg Wächter

--All signed next to each other.

PENNSYLVANIA RECORDS:

Warwick Lutheran KB, Lancaster County, Pennsylvania:

Laurently Haushalter had baptized:
1. Margaretha, born 4 July 1754, baptized 28 July 1754, sp. Georg Hakker & Margaretha Weidmennin
2. Jacob, born 30 Sep 1761, baptized 18 Oct 1761, sp. Jacob Weidmann & his wife
3. Barbara, born 4 Nov 1763, baptized 24 Trinity 1763, sp. Jacob Weidmann & his wife
4. Catharina, born 17 Feb 1766, baptized 21 Feb 1766, sp. Joh. Adam Haker
5. Johann Jacob, born 19 Feb 1767, baptized Estomihi 1767
6. Elisabeth, born 6 Jan 1768, baptized 13 Jan 1768, sp. Adam Haker & his wife
7. Gottlieb, born 26 Jul 1770 baptized 29 Jul 1770, sp. Adam Hacker & his wife Elisabeth
8. Christina, born 4 Mar 1772, baptized 19 Apr 1772, sp. Adam Hacker & his wife Elisabeth
9. Susanna, born 14 Sep 1774, baptized 18 Sep 1774, sp. Adam Hacker & his wife Elisabeth

Lorentz Hausshalter & his wife sponsored child of Michael Lang on 13 Nov 1757
Lorentz Haushalter & his wife sponsored child of Jacob Weidman on [Oct 1762]
Lorentz Haushalter & his wife sponsored child of Ulrich Bekle on Festival of the Ascension 1763

Lorentz Haushalter & his wife sponsored children of Johann Adam Hacker on 12 Oct 1766, 29 Nov 1768, and 27 Jan 1771

Confirmed Trinity I 1780:
Barbara Haushalterin
Catharina Haushalterin

Lancaster County, Pennsylvania, Estate Records:

Lancaster Will I-202:
Lawrence Householder, yeoman, of Cocalico Township, writ 19 Jul 1800, probated 12 Feb 1805.
1. "being old and weak"
2. He makes provisions for his wife Margaret, who may continue to reside in the old room of the house they now live in for the rest of her natural life.
3. To my son Jacob: My horse creature.
4. To each of my two daughters Elizabeth and Susanna: One cow to make them equal with my other children.
5. To my son Jacob Householder: All that my plantation and tract of land whereon I now live containing about 117 acres and adjoining to lands of Christopher Oberlin, George Weidman, John Watcher, Christopher Miller, and others.
6. The value of my real estate estate is to be divided equally among my children, viz.: Jacob, Barbara (intermarried with Frederick Adam), Catharine (intermarried with George Stober), Elizabeth, Susanna, and the heirs of my deceased daughter Margaret.
7. If my son Jacob should die without lawful heirs (the word issue is lined out), then my plantation shall fall back unto my other children, to be equally divided amongst them.
8. The residue of my estate to be equally divided amongst my aforesaid children.
9. Executors: My son Jacob and my trusty friend George Weidman.
10. Signed his name as Lawrence Householder.
11. Witnessed by Frederick Hocker and John W. Sauter.

Martin Jock (or Jogg)

1739 Friendship

In 1737, Martin Jock, the widow Elisabeth Becher, and Johann Haushalter requested permission to emigrate. The applications of Jock and Haushalter were rejected.

Martin Jock and Johann Adam Haushalter (q.v.) arrived at Philadelphia in 1739 aboard the Ship *Friendship*. This Adam Haushalter was the son of the said Johann Haushalter who--in 1725-- married Maria Elisabeth, daughter of Georg Jock, as his second wife.

Johann Haushalter disappears from Russheim records after 1739. It would seem that he and his wife Maria Elisabeth went to Pennsylvania with their children. Perhaps Johann Haushalter died during passage and his widow Elisabeth arrived on the Ship *Friendship* with her brother Martin Jock.

GERMAN RECORDS:

Russheim Evangelisch KB:

George Jogg, son of Hans Andreas Jogg , married 11 Aug 1705 Anna, daughter (?) of Georg Steinmetz

Georg Jock (alias Jogg) & his wife Anna had baptized:
1. Elisabetha, baptized 8 July 1706
2. Johann Martin, baptized 12 Sep 1707 (see Bild 20)
3. Margaretha, born 26 July 1711

Married 27 Nov 1725: Johannes Haushalter, widower (wittwer), and Maria Elisabetha, daughter of Georg Jock

Married 17 May 1729: Johann Martin Jock, son of Georg, to Maria Moogin, daughter of Henrich Moog. Pastor's notation: "Went to the New Land 1739."

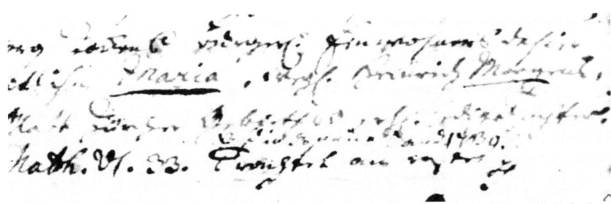

Above: The pastor wrote "they went to the new land 1739" next to their marriage record. Landeskirchliches Archiv Karlsruhe > Rußheim > Mischbuch 1692 - 1738 - Bild 63 (Accessed via Archion.de)

Martin Jock, citizen, and his wife Maria, born Moogin, had baptized:
1. Christina, born 6 Feb 1730
2. Michael, born 10 Aug 1731, baptized 12 Aug 1731—died 10 Aug 1731
3. Maria Catharina, born 19 Sep 1733—died 21 Sep 1733

IMMIGRATION:

Hacker, *Auswanderung aus Baden und dem Breisgau:*

Hacker Emigrant 4623:
Martin Jock, Russheim. Emigration application rejected. 1737.

Ship *Friendship*, qualified 3 Sep 1739 at Philadelphia:

Martin (O) Yoak, age 31
John Philip (+) Herberger [not found on List A]
Hans Adam ([) Hausholder, age 20

PENNSYLVANIA RECORDS:

Lancaster County, Pennsylvania, Estate Records:

Lancaster Will C405:
Martin Yock (his mark: X), yeoman, of Earl tp., writ 25 Mar 1776, probated 5 Nov 1776
1. To his daughter Christina, the wife of Michael Difendorfer: A monetary bequest.
2. He devises the residue of his estate unto "all my grandchildren," that is, the children of his said daughter Christina, excepting Adam Diller who has already received his inheritance. The grandchildren are not to receive their shares until each comes of age.
3. Executor: Grandson Adam Diller
4. Witnessed by George Dietrich, Henrich Bauman, and Emanuel Carpenter.

New Holland Lutheran KB, Lancaster County, Pennsylvania:

Hans Martin Diller m. 8 Apr 1746 Christina Jack

Martin Diller & his wife Christina Maria Magdalena, born Jokin (but given as born Martin for the first child), had baptized:
1. Philip Adam, b. 31 Jan 1751, sp. Adam Diller & Maria Magdalena
2. Johann Jacob, b. 16 May 1754, sp. Jacob Difendorder & Anna Maria Dillerin

Martin Jock & his wife Maria sponsored child of Balthasar Lawer [Laber] & his wife Elisabeth, born Baumann, on 5 Aug 1759

Communicants 25 May 1765:
Martin Jook
Anna Maria Jokin

Communicants 19 Apr 1767: Mart. Jock
Communicants 19 Trinity 1768: Martin Jok (also appears on other list to 18 May 1771)
Communicants 13 May 1769: Mart. Jock
Communicants 15 Apr 1770: Mart. Jock
Communicants 29 Oct 1770: Mart. Jock
Communicants 18 May 1771: Martin Jock

Lancaster (Trinity) Lutheran KB, Lancaster, Lancaster County, Pennsylvania:

Buried 16 Aug 1795 in the Reformed churchyard, our Widow Christine Tieffendörfer, aged 67 years

Wendel Keller

1749 Ann

Wendel Keller married the widow Barbara Schmidt of Russheim in 1749. At the time of marriage, he was a resident of Liedolsheim. Unfortunately, the Liedolsheim records prior to 1734 are not extant. In his last will & testament, he does make a bequest to stepbrothers and stepsisters residing in Germany.

Friederich and Barbara Schmidt's children also went to America in 1749. I have chosen to analyze them separately in this volume.

GERMAN RECORDS:

Russheim Evangelisch KB:

Married 22 May 1749: Wendel Keller of Liedolsheim and Barbara Schmidt, the widow of Friederich Schmid.

The marriage record (see below) is difficult to read on microfilm. The marriage of Henrich Mock and the Widow Elser (q.v.) appears just above this entry. See the Elser family analysis, which includes notes from the pastor that the widows Elser and Schmidt about concerns in the community over the intended emigration of the mothers and the inheritances of their children.

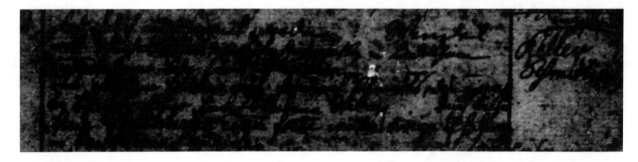

Landeskirchliches Archiv Karlsruhe > Rußheim > Mischbuch 1738 - 1777,Apr. 1800,1817 - Bild 239 (Accessed via Archion.de)

IMMIGRATION:

Ship *Ann*, qualified 28 Sep 1749 at Philadelphia:

Wendel (WK) Keller

PENNSYLVANIA RECORDS:

Stoever, Rev. John Casper, personal register:

George Wendel Keller married 18 Dec 1753 Barbara Straup, Bethel

Wendel Keller married 4 July 1756 Elisabeth Fuchs. Bethel

Married 14 Mar 1757 in Lebanon: Wendel Keller and Catharina Dorothea Haberlandin

Wendel Keller (Lebanon) had baptized:
1. Jacobina Rosina, born 14 Nov 1761, baptized 29 Nov 1761, sp. Michael Laurie & his wife
2. George Wendel, born July 1764, baptized 24 July 1764, sp. Michael Balmer & his wife

For further research: A Wendel Keller, born 1760, died 1760, appears on a memorial stone in Hebron Moravian Cemetery.

Lancaster County, Pennsylvania, Estate Records:

Lancaster Will B604:
Wendel Keller, taylor, of Lebanon Town, writ 7 Jan 1771, probated 23 Feb 1771.
1. "being at present sick and weak of body"
2. My executors are to sell my house and lot situate in Lebanon Town for the best price.
3. To my only beloved daughter Jacobina Rosina Keller: All my estate.
4. My executors "shall bring up maintain and educate" my said daughter.
5. If my daughter should die under age and without issue, then my estate shall be divided as follows:
    a. To Michael Lowrey: The sum of five pounds.
    b. The residue divided into two equal parts:
        i. One part to my stepbrother Philip Aible.
        ii. The other part to my sister Catharine the wife of a certain Warm [sic]
6. He identifies his stepbrother and his sister as residents of the Empire of Germany.
7. Executors: Trusty friends Conrad Renninger and Michael Lowry.
8. Signed his name with a mark.
9. Witnessed by John Jacob Sautter and Christian Frendling.

Lancaster Orphans Court, proceedings dated 23 Feb 1771:
Wendel Keller, decd., late of Lebanon tp. (260)
Minor Child: Rosina Keller (under 14)--the court appoints Michael Lowrey of the same place as her guardian.

Note: A Wendel Keller taxed 1780 to 1789 in Heidelberg Township, York County, Pennsylvania.

Diebold Lang and his son Michael Lang

1737 William (Diebold Lang)
1752 Rawley (Michael Lang)

Marital discord existed then as now. Diebold Lang of Russheim appears to have abandoned his wife Margaretha Neess and absconded to Pennsylvania, where he raised another family. His son Michael Lang of Russheim arrived in 1752. It is uncertain as to whether father and son had any formal relationship at all in Pennsylvania.

In Pennsylvania, son Michael Lang first settled among other Russheimers and Baden-Durlach emigrants, where he frequently interacted with them in church records.

GERMAN RECORDS:

Russheim Evangelisch KB:

Married 7 Aug 1721: Johann Diebold Lang and Margaretha, geboren Neessin

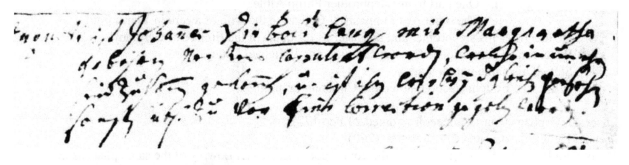

Landeskirchliches Archiv Karlsruhe > Rußheim > Mischbuch 1692 - 1738 - Bild 62 (Accessed via Archion.de)

Hans Diebold (or Theobald) Lang & his wife Margaretha, born Neessin, had baptized:
1. Johann Michael, born 29 Nov 1721
2. Lorentz, born 8 Apr 1726—gestorben Feb 1805

Johann Debold Lang & his wife Maria Barbara had baptized:
3. Peter, born 24 Aug 1724, baptized 25 Aug 1724—died 30 Aug 1724

Note: A daughter Margaretha Lang should have been born to Theobald Lang circa 1730 to 1734—if Pennsylvania records are correct. I did not see a baptism for a child in this time frame. Further: Diebold Lang's wife's given name is distinct in the baptismal record for son Peter—but the pastor made no mention of an illegitimate child. Perhaps the pastor errantly recorded the mother's name.

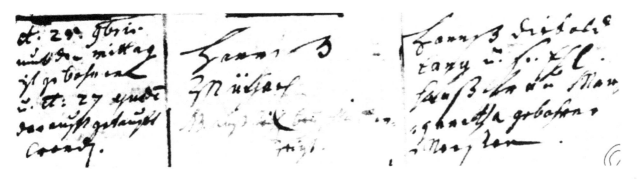

Above: 1721 Russheim baptismal record for Michael Lang, son of Hans Diebold Lang. Landeskirchliches Archiv Karlsruhe > Rußheim > Mischbuch 1692 - 1738 - Bild 41 (Accessed via Archion.de)

Important: I cannot read the notation made by the pastor under Hans Michael's name in the above baptism. It indicates that the children went somewhere—but I cannot make out all the letters.

Married 8 Nov 1746: Johann Micheal Lang and Christina Hacker. (Note: I am taking this date from other researchers. On the microfilm record available to me, the marriages near this date are too darkened to read. I can make out "Michael.")

Joh. Michael Lang and his wife Christina, nee Hacker, had baptized:
1. Johann Georg, born 6 Nov 1747, baptized 6 Nov 1747
2. Christina, born 18 Dec 1751, baptized 18 Dec 1751 (Pastor's notation: "went to the new land")

Note: I checked all baptisms between 1747 and 1751 but did not locate another child born to this couple.

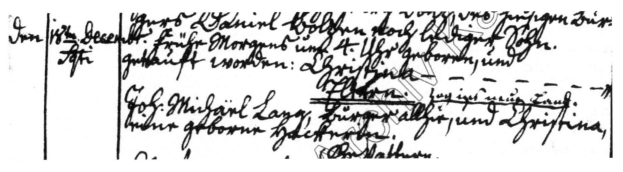

Above: The pastor wrote "went to the new land" (zog im neue land) after the German word Eltern (parents). Landeskirchliches Archiv Karlsruhe > Rußheim > Mischbuch 1738 - 1777, Apr. 1800, 1817 - Bild 31 (Accessed via Archion.de)

The baptismal record below (see image) is of great importance to Lang researchers. Among the baptismal sponsors for a child of Friederich Boltz is "Margaretha, wife of Diebold Langen, in Pensylvanien, born Neessin." I interpret this as *Margaretha, the wife of Diebold Lang of Pennsylvania*. Surely Margaretha was present at the child's baptism—while her husband was presumably in Pennsylvania.

It seems as if the Lang family separated. The father likely went to Pennsylvania in 1737 (a Diebold Lang signed next to Russheim emigrant Michael Neess [q.v.] on the passenger list of the Ship *William* that year). He is surely the same person who appears in New Hanover Lutheran records with a wife named

Anna Maria. In his last will and testament, dated 1777, he identified eldest son Michael and next lists son Lorentz. These names match the oldest surviving children of the Diebold Lang of Rußheim.

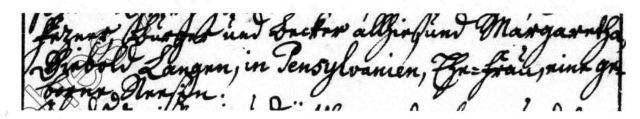

Above: Note the word "Pensylvanien" after Diebold Langen's name. Landeskirchliches Archiv Karlsruhe > Rußheim > Mischbuch 1738 - 1777, Apr. 1800,1817 - Bild 28 (Accessed via Archion.de)

Died 15 Dec 1755: Margaretha Langin, wife of Theobald Lang, who has left her and it is not certain whether he is living, aged 63 years, 10 months, age 28 days

IMMIGRATION:

Researcher Kris Hocker has viewed the Russheim Ortsippenbuch. In the record for Diebold Lang, she found the following: "Bem: hat 1735 boshafterweise seine Ehefrau verlassen. Ober aber noch lebt ist nicht gewiss." Loosely translated: In 1735 he wickedly left his wife. It is not certain whether or not he is still alive."

Hacker, *Auswanderung aus Baden und dem Breisgau:*

Hacker Emigrant 5985:
Hans Michael Lang of Russheim, with wife and two children. Manumitted 7 March 1752 along with Christof Hacker. Intends to go to America.

Ship *William*, qualified 31 Oct 1737 at Philadelphia:

Johan Michel Neess
Theobald (X) Lange
--Signed next to each other.

Ship *Rawley*, qualified 23 Oct 1752 at Philadelphia:

Hans Jerg Steidinger
Johan Philip (X) Frech
George (X) Brown
Johannes Seitz
Lorentz (X) Houshalter
Joseph Burgstahler
Christoph Hacker

Michel Lang
Matheas (X) Miller
Hans Jorg Mock
Hans Jorg Wächter
--All signed next to each other.

Naturalized (Pennsylvania) 17 Oct 1765: Theobald Long, Colebrookdale, Berks County

PENNSYLVANIA RECORDS:

New Hanover Lutheran KB, Montgomery County, Pennsylvania

(selected records)

Theobald Lang & his wife Anna Maria had baptized:
1. Eva Rosina, born 2 June 1747, baptized 9 Aug 1747, sp. Stephen Hauck & his wife Eva Rosina

Peter Lange & his wife Catharina had baptized:
1. Peter, born 15 July 1769, baptized 10 Sep 1769, sp. Theobald Lang & his wife Anna Maria

Theobald Lang & his wife Anna Maria sponsored child of Daniel Böhme & his wife Margaretha on 13 Dec 1775

Peter Lange & his wife Catharina sponsored child of Daniel Böhme & his wife Margaretha on 10 Sep 1769

Confirmed 5 Nov 1749:
Anna Margareth Lang, Theobald Lang's daughter, age 17 years

Confirmed 21 Apr 1754:
Peter Lange, Theobald Lange's son, age 15 years
Daniel Böhm, Theobald Lange's stepson, in his 16th year
Anna Maria Lange, Theobald Lange's daughter, aged 14 years

Peter Lange, died 26 Oct 1776, aged 37 years, 1 month, 2 weeks, and 5 days

Oley Hill Church KB, Berks County, Pennsylvania:

Rudolph Dotter, Ref., married 31 Jan 1758 Catharina Lang, daughter of Theobald Lang

Warwick Lutheran KB, Lancaster County, Pennsylvania:

(selected only)

Michael Lang had baptized:
1. Johann Michael, born 15 Oct 1757, baptized 15 Nov 1757, sp. Lorentz Hausshalter & his wife

Confirmed 1771 on the First Easter Day: Mich. Lang, age 14 years, son of Mich. Lang

Georg Lang had baptized:
1. Anna Rosina, born 1 June 1765, baptized 3 Trinity 1765, sp. Conrad Lang & his wife
2. Elisabetha, born 12 Mar 1767, baptized Quasimodogeniti 1767, sp. Peter Beinhauer & Elisabetha Millerin
3. Maria Barbara, born 16 Aug 1768, baptized [not given], sp. Peter Beinhauer & Barbara Stoberin
4. Johannes, born 15 Sep 1771, baptized 10 Nov 1771, sp. Conrad Lange & his wife Anna

--Mother identified as Gertraut at 1771 baptism.

Georg Lange & his wife sponsored child of Peter Maerkel on 1 Mar 1772

Conrad Lang & his wife Anna Rosina had baptized:
1. Elisabetha, born 28 Dec 1765, baptized 2 Feb 1766, sp. Wolffgang Schmezer
2. Anna Rosina, born 1 Feb 1767, baptized 15 Mar 1766 [sic], sp. William Hag & his wife
3. Anna Maria, born 12 Feb 1773, baptized 2 May 1773, sp. Joh. Karch & his wife Catharina

Note: The George Lang above may not be Michael Lang's son born in Germany. No connection between Michael Lang (the Father) and the Conrad Lang has been identified.

Lancaster County, Tax Records, 1751-1789:

Michael Lang, Cocalico Township 1756-1763, inmate (laborer '59)
Michael Lang, Cocalico Township, 1779-1789+, 60A to 160A

I have compiled tax abstracts for adjoining townships Warwick, Cocalico, and Elizabeth for all years available between 1751 and 1789. The only Michael Langs appearing are noted above. The older Michael Lang is surely the emigrant from Russheim. He did not own property. The years 1764 to 1768 are not extant. He may have died. The other Michael Lang is presumably his son. The father should appear in tax lists from 1769 to 1778—but an index of Pennsylvania tax lists for that time period shows no Michael Lang/Long. Perhaps the father died or became ineligible for taxation.

Berks County, Pennsylvania, Estate Files (go to image 651 on familysearch.org):

Last will and testament of Deobolt Long of Colebrookdale Twp., Philadelphia County, yeoman, writ 21 Aug 1777; proved 11 Apr 1780.
1. He makes provisions for his wife Anna Mary.
2. To my eldest son Michael: 20 shillings lawful money of Pennsylvania.
3. To my son Lawrence Long: 20 shillings lawful money of Pennsylvania.

4. To the heirs of my son Peter Long, late deceased: The sum of five shillings lawful money of Pennsylvania (over and above all that what my said son Peter Long hath already received of me).
5. To my daughter Catherine the wife of Michael Dotterer: The sum of 10 pounds lawful money of Pennsylvania.
6. To my daughter Mary: The sum of five shillings lawful money of Pennsylvania.
7. To my daughter Eve the wife of Abraham Danner: The sum of three pounds lawful money of Pennsylvania.
8. To my stepson Daniel Boehm: The sum of five shillings lawful money of Pennsylvania.
9. Daughters: Catharine wife of Michael Dotterer, Mary, and Eve wife of Abraham Danner.
10. Executor: son-in-law Abraham Danner.
11. Witnesses: Peter Richards, John Eckiss, and George Shiner.
12. Source: Berks County, Pennsylvania, Will Abstracts, Will Book B., p. 24.

Berks County, Pennsylvania, Deed B1-245: Theobald Long, yeoman, of Colebrookdale Township enfrel.to his son Peter Long, yeoman, of the same place

150A Colebrookdale Township: HISTORY: 150A Colebrookdale Township surveyed unto John Conrad Behme in pursuance of a warrant dated 15 July 1734. By an agreement dated 2 Apr 1736, John Conrad Behme assigned his right to the same to one John Behme. Thereafter, John Behme died leaving issue an only son and heir named Daniel Behme. On 16 Feb 1760, Daniel Behme granted his right and title to Theobald Long, the first party hereto. // On 8 Mar 1749, the said Theobald Long—by the name of Dewalt Long--obtained a new warrant for the aforesaid property, vacating the original warrant given to John Conrad Behme. (Note: Theobald Long signed the indenture with the initials JDL.)

--5 Apr 1768

Veit Müller

1739 Friendship

Scores of German emigrants left their homeland without permission. I find no evidence of Veit Müller in Russheim emigration records; however, the facts below suggest that the Veit Müller, born Anno 1714 in Russheim, left for America in 1739 and took up residence in Lancaster County, Pennsylvania. Note that Veit's sister Elisabeth married Joseph Burgstahler in 1732. Their son Joseph Burgstahler arrived in Pennsylvania in 1752.

GERMAN RECORDS:

Russheim Evangelisch KB:

Married 17 May 1707: Daniel Muller, son of Jacob Muller, and Margaretha Geckenheimer, daughter of Johann Michael Geckenheimer

Daniel Miller & his wife Anna Margaretha had baptized:
1. Johann Michael, baptized 29 Mar 1708—died 22 June 1740
2. Anna Elisabetha, born 10 Apr 1710, baptized 11 Apr 1710
3. Hans Veit, born 8 Jan 1714, baptized 9 Jan 1714
4. Johann Friederich, born 7 Sep 1716, baptized 8 Sep 1716—died 11 May 1724
5. Daniel, born 17 July 1721, baptized 17 July 1721—died 15 Feb 1723
6. Catharina Barbara, born 29 Mar 1726

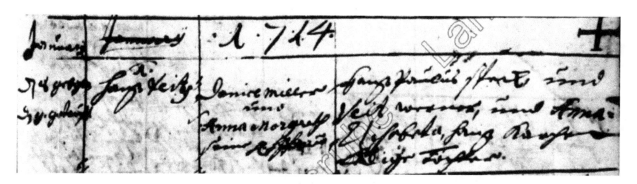

Above: 1714 baptism of Hans Veit Muller. Landeskirchliches Archiv Karlsruhe > Rußheim > Mischbuch 1692 - 1738 - Bild 30 (Accessed via Archion.de)

Died 27 Feb 1731: Daniel Muller, aged 48 years

Married 6 May 1732: Joseph Burgstaller and Elisabetha Muller, daughter of Daniel Muller

Note: See the section on Russheim emigrant Joseph Burgstahler (q.v.).

IMMIGRATION:

Ship *Friendship*, qualified 3 Sep 1739 at Philadelphia:

Frantz Brossman, age 45
Michael (X) Floris [not in this position on List A]
<u>Veit Miller, age 25</u>
Christian (X) Ergott, age 25
Henrich Heyl, age 40

Note: Russheimers Martin Jock (q.v.) and Adam Haushalter (q.v.) also on this ship.

PENNSYLVANIA RECORDS:

Lancaster Moravian KB, Lancaster, Lancaster County, Pennsylvania:

Married 21 Feb 1744: Vitus Müller and Anna Maria Schweichin

Lancaster Reformed KB, Lancaster, Lancaster County, Pennsylvania:

Veit Muller & Anna Maria Muller had baptized:
1. Andreas, baptized 3 Feb 1745, sp. Andrew Beyrle
2. Anna Maria, born 27 Jan 1751, baptized 5 May 1751, sp. Philip Edinger & his wife
3. Margaretha, born 11 May 1754, baptized 30 June 1754, sp. Adam Schuesseler &his wife

Veit Muller's wife Anna Maria sponsored child of Philip Edinger & his wife Anna Maria on 15 July 1750

Lancaster Lutheran KB, Lancaster, Lancaster County, Pennsylvania:

Buried 21 January 1794 in our churchyard, an old member of the congregation, Veit Müller, aged 80 years and 12 days

Adam Nees and his son Johannes Nees

1749 Ann

Nearly all persons surnamed Nees in Lancaster County, Pennsylvania, can be traced to Russheim. Most are children or descendants of Sebastian Nees (q.v.). However, there are some Lancaster Nees records that do not fit into that family. I suspect these persons are connected to 1749 Russheim emigrant Adam Nees. Further research is necessary.

GERMAN RECORDS:

Russheim Lutheran KB:

Johann Adam Neess & his wife Anna Margaretha had baptized:
1. Johann Georg, born 8 Aug 1704
2. Johann Adam, born 4 June 1706
3. Maria Margaretha, born 1h9 Nov 1708—died 28 Dec 1749
4. Maria Barbara, bp. 27 Jan 1714
5. Joh. Michael, bp. 30 Jan 1717

--Note: The microfilm is too dark to read son Adam's baptismal entry. I have taken the birth date from the German IGI. Another Adam Nees had a son baptized in 1699. A cross is next to that child's name. That Adam may be the Adam Nees, son of Adam Nees, who married Catharina Hacker in 1737. This couple remained in Russheim. The baptismal entry for the 1699 Adam Nees has a cross next to the child's name, indicating he died in the vicinity.

Married 4 May 1728: Joh. Adam Neess, son of Johann Adam Neessin, and Margaretha, daughter of (Joh.?) Werner [see image below]

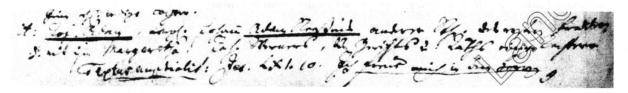

Landeskirchliches Archiv Karlsruhe > Rußheim > Mischbuch 1692 - 1738 - Bild 63

Johann Adam Neess & his wife Margaretha, born Wernerin, had baptized:
1. Johannes, born 21 June 1729
2. Johann Georg, born 7 Nov 1730
3. Johann Friedrich, born 14 Aug 1732, baptized 15 Aug 1732—cross next to child's name
4. Catharina, born 30 Jan 1736, baptized 31 Jan 1736
5. Johann Adam, born 1 Jan 1740
6. Johann Michael, born 1 Oct 1742—died 26 Jan 1749
7. Christina, born 21 July 1745—died 21 May 1746

--Note: I reviewed baptisms recorded between 1731-1735 and 1737-1739 several times. Some pages are difficult to read. There may be another child or children born to this couple in Russheim.

Hans Adam Neess, son of Hans Adam Neess, married 15 Jan 1737 Anna Catharina Hackerin, daughter of Georg Hacker. They had baptized:
1. Johann Adam, born 30 Nov 1739, baptized 1 Jan 1740
2. Johann Adam, born 28 Nov 1740—died 14 July 1816

--Note: This couple had other children born in Russheim. Nearly all had notations of death beside their names, indicating that this family remained in Russheim. Therefore, the 1749 Russheim emigrant Adam Neess must be the man who married Margaretha Werner.

IMMIGRATION:

Hacker Emigrant 7291:
Joh. Adam Neess of Russheim, with wife and four children. Intends to go to America. Manumitted 18 March 1749.

Ship *Ann*, qualified 28 Sep 1749 at Philadelphia:

Hans Adam Nees
Hans Nes

PENNSYLVANIA RECORDS:

Lancaster (Trinity) Lutheran KB, Lancaster County, Pennsylvania:

Married 24 June 1766: Johann Adam Naess, single, and Catharina Hohnin, single.

Maytown Lutheran KB, Lancaster County, Pennsylvania:

Adam Nass & his wife Catharine had baptized:
1. Bernhard, b. 25 Mar 1767, sp. Bernhard Speck (q.v.) & wife Magdalena
2. Magdalena, b. 22 Apr 1772, sp. Grandmother Maria Magdalena Hens
3. Joh. Jacob, b. 30 May 1773, sp. Joh. Jacob Wolf & wife Barbara
4. Catharina, b. 6 Jul 1775, sp. Jacob Wolf & wife Barbara
5. Michael, b. 14 Jan 1779, sp. Abraham Lang & wife Maria Magdalena
6. Daniel, b. 23 Jan 1780, sp. Heinrich Hans

Joh. Adam Nees & his wife Catharine sponsored child of Bernhard Speck & his wife Magdalena on 12 Jul 1767
Adam Nass & his wife Catharine sponsored child of Jacob Wolf & his wife Barbara on 17 Oct 1772
Adam Nass & his wife Catharine sponsored child of Johannes Nicholas & his wife Eva on 10 Nov 1772

Maytown Reformed KB, Lancaster County, Pennsylvania:

Adam Nees & his wife Catharine had baptized:
1. Johann Adam, b. 29 Jan 1770, sp. Bernhard Speck & wife Magdalena
2. Johannes, b. 4 Feb 1782, sp. Parents

For consideration:

The following wills link together four siblings: Catharina Nees, Adam Nees, Jacob Nees, and John Nees. Are they related to Adam Nees and Margaretha Werner of Russheim?

Lancaster Will H352:
Catharine Mead, widow, of Cocalico Township, writ 4 July 1796, probated 11 Aug 1803.
1. To Philip Rahn, Jr., the son of Philip Rahn, Sr.: The sum of ten pounds.
2. To Philip Road, Sr.: The sum of five pounds "of like money according to a former will made by my first husband John Shotter."
3. To Elizabeth, daughter of Adam Nees, deceased: Five of my best shifts.
4. To Elizabeth Killian: Five of my best shifts "for many favours she has done me in my Life Time."
5. To my two brothers John Nees and Jacob Nees: The remainder of my estate, both real and personal.
6. Executors: Brother John Nees and loving friend Philip Rahn.
7. Witnessed by Adam Mosser, Marcus Montelius, and William Shoemaker.
8. Signed her name with a mark.

Lancaster Will I-371:
Adam Nees, yeoman, of Rapho Township, writ 16 Mar 1803, probated 3 Jan 1806.
1. He makes provisions for his wife Margaret.
2. He authorizes his executors to sell and dispose of all my real estate for the advantage of his children. The profits are to be divided amongst his children, to wit: John Nees, George Nees, Adam Nees, Samuel Nees, Catharine (the wife of Jacob Stover), Hannah (the wife of Conrad Meinser), and Susanna Nees.
3. He makes provisions to ensure that the share of his daughter Catharine shall not come into the control of her husband Jacob Stover. If she should die with issue a child or children, then her share shall go to them. If she should die childless, then her share to be divided amongst the testator's other children.
4. Executors: Sons John Nees and George Nees.
5. Witnessed by John Stom and Peter Blattenberger.
6. Signed his name as Adam Nees.

Lancaster Will I-374:
John Nees, yeoman, of the Borough of Lancaster, writ 21 Aug 1793, probated 5 Nov 1807.
1. To my eldest brother Adam Nees: The sum of five pounds. He further forgives debts that the said Adam owes unto him.
2. To my nephew John Nees (son of my said brother): The sum of ten pounds.
3. To my brother Jacob Nees: The sum of ten pounds.
4. To the poor of the Religious Society of People or Congregation to which I belong settled and establish in the township of Cocalico in the said county of Lancaster: The sum of five pounds.
5. To the Superintendents for the time being of the burial ground where I may happen to be interred: The sum of five pounds to be applied for and towards repairing such burial ground and the enclosure thereof.
6. To my beloved wife Salome: All and singular my lands, messuages, tenements, hereditaments, and real estate whatsoever and wheresoever as well as the residue of my personal estate.
7. Executors: Wife Salome and my trusty friend William Dischong of Cocalico Township.

8. Witnessed by Jacob Mayer and Philip Gloninger.
9. Signed his name as John Nees.
10. Codicil dated 17 Jan 1807: As the said William Dishong is now deceased, I appoint my trusty friend George Hensel of the Borough of Lancaster in his place.

Michael Nees

1737 William

The family of Michael Nees' father, Sebastian Nees (q.v.), migrated to America, settling in the vicinity of Cocalico Township, Lancaster County. It appears that Michael went first, as his father and siblings arrived at the Colonies a year after him.

GERMAN RECORDS:

Russheim Evangelisch KB:

Bastian Neess & his wife Anna of Russheim, near Karlsruhe in Baden, had baptized:
1. Johann Michael, baptized 15 Mar 1706

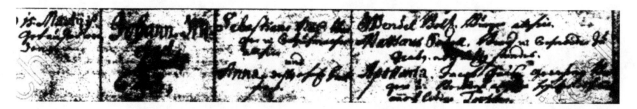

Above: 1706 baptism of Michael Nees. Landeskirchliches Archiv Karlsruhe > Rußheim > Mischbuch 1692 - 1738 - Bild 18 (Accessed via Archion.de)

Married 29 Nov 1729: Johann Michael, son of Sebastian Nees, married Elisabetha, daughter of Sebastian Hager.

Johann Michael Neess & his wife Elisabetha, nee Hagerin, had baptized:
1. Joh. Georg, born 11 Jan 1731, baptized 13 Jan 1731--died 5 July 1734
2. Maria Barbara, born 3 Apr 1733
3. Johann Michael, born 2 Oct 1734, baptized 3 Oct 1734
4. Hans Georg, born 1 Oct 1736

IMMIGRATION:

Hacker, *Auswanderung aus Baden und dem Breisgau:*

Hacker Emigrant 7274:
Michael Neff [sic: Neess], Russheim, went to Pennsylvania. He and Martin Weidmann of Graben reside in Pennsylvania. They are to receive the inheritance of Margaret Winacher [sic: Reinacher], the wife of Georg Albert in Pennsylvania. Dated 23 July 1748.

Hacker Emigrant 7290:
Joh. Michael Neess of Russheim, will go to Pennsylvania. Manumitted 13 February 1737.

Ship *William*, qualified 31 Oct 1737 at Philadelphia:

Johan Michel Neess
Theobald (X) Lange (q.v.)

--Signed next to each other.

PENNSYLVANIA RECORDS:

Muddy Creek Lutheran KB, East Cocalico Township, Lancaster County, Pennsylvania:

Michael Näss had baptized:
1. Maria Catharina, b. 3 Jan 1738, sp. Joh. George Buch & Maria Elisabeth Weidmannin
2. Joh. Adam, b. 4 Sep 1740, sp. Joh. George Buch & his wife
3. Catharina Elisabeth, b. 8 Mar 1742, sp. George Buch & his wife

Michael Nass & Agnes Reuterin sponsored child of Stephan Braun on 10 Apr 1743

Sebastian Nass and Elisabeth Nass, Michael Nass's wife, sponsored child of Joh. George Konig of Tulpehocken on 27 Dec 1739

Joh. Martin Oberlin & Maria Catharina Nassin sponsored child of David Hager on 19 Jan 1741

New Holland Lutheran KB, Lancaster County, Pennsylvania:

Married 26 Feb 1765: Adam Nehs, son of the late Michael, and Margreta Oberle, daughter of Michael, were married at home.

Married 23 Jan 1766: Henrich Martin, widower, and Eva Nehs, daughter of the late Michael, both from Cocalico, were married at Adam Nehs.

Lancaster (Trinity) Lutheran KB, Lancaster County, Pennsylvania:

Communion, Easter, 1751:
178. Michael Naess, Cocalico tp.
179. Elisabeth Naessen

Lancaster County, Pennsylvania, Estate Records:

Lancaster County Estate Index:
Michael Neass, 1761, testate, Will Y2-496
Michael Nease, 1761, intestate

Lancaster County Orphans Court Proceedings dated 6 Mar 1771:
Estate of MICHAEL NEISS, decd., late of Cocalico tp. (page 268)
--Executor Adam Neiss produces an account. The court approves the balances and ordered to distributed according to the intentions of the last will and testament; viz., to the widow [not named] and children Adam, Elizabeth, Margaret, Eve, Mary, Christina, Magdalena, and Catharine

Sebastian Nees (or Neess)

1738 Friendship

Many families migrated in stages. It appears that Sebastian's Nees's son Michael (q.v.) departed Russheim in 1737. His father Sebastian and siblings followed a year later.

GERMAN RECORDS:

Russheim Evangelisch KB:

Bastian Neess & his wife Anna of Russheim, near Karlsruhe in Baden, had baptized:
2. Johann Michael, baptized 15 Mar 1706
3. Anna Elisabetha, born 10 Apr 1709, baptized 11 Apr 1709—died 13 Apr 1709
4. Anna Elisabetha, born 11 Sep 1710, baptized 12 Sep 1710—died 23 Aug 1717
5. Bastian, bp. 13 Aug 1713—died 10 June 1720
6. Margaretha, bp. 13 Jul 1716
7. Maria Barbara, bp. 27 Jan 1720
8. Anna Catharina, bp. 23 Jan 1722

Died 18 July 1725: Anna, wife of Sebastian Neesin, aged 44 years

Married 29 Oct 1726: Sebastian Neess, widower, and Catharina Barbara, daughter of Johann Michael Bechtel (?--I have trouble reading the German name—see image below.)

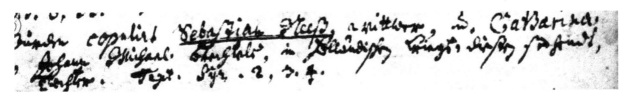

Landeskirchliches Archiv Karlsruhe > Rußheim > Mischbuch 1692 - 1738 - Bild 62 (Access via Archion.de)

Sebastian Neess & his wife Catharina had baptized:
1. Anna, born 13 May 1728, baptized 15 May 1728
2. Sebastian, born 26 Jan 1730, baptized 26 Jan 1730—died 5 Feb 1730

Died 5 Feb 1730: Sebastian, son of Sebastian Nees and his wife Catharina, aged 9 days
Died 5 Feb 1730: Catharina, wife of Sebastian Nees, born Bechtlin (Berchtlin?) aged 25 years, 2 months, and 13 days

IMMIGRATION:

Ship *Friendship*, qualified 20 Sep 1738 at Philadelphia:

Fridrig Karle, age 26 (signed his name)
Sebastian (X) Neas, age 55
Henrich Hernner, age 46
Geo. Daniel (X) Gesmer, age 45
Veit Bechtoldt, age 26

PENNSYLVANIA RECORDS:

Warwick Lutheran KB, Elizabeth Township, Lancaster County, Pennsylvania:

Joh. Martin Oberlin m. 25 June 1739 Anna Margaretha Nassin
Joh. Heinrich Motz m. 20 Nov 1739 Barbara Nassin
Joh. Jacob Stober m. 1 Feb 1743 Anna Catharina Nassin

Married 24 Feb 1743: Sebastian Nass and Margaretha Bruain (Note: Her surname given as Grossin in my translation of the Muddy Creek Register. I do not have access to the original book.)

Sebastian Näss had baptized:
1. Sebastian, b. 31 May 1745, sp. Joh. Georg Huber & his wife Anna Maria

Sebastian Nass & wife sponsored child of Joh. George Huber on 23 Mar 1746 and 17 Jan 1748

Lancaster Moravian KB, Lancaster County, Pennsylvania

Married 13 Mar 1744: Hans George Naes and Marg. Eichelberger

Lancaster County, Pennsylvania, Estate Records:

Lancaster Estate Index:
Sebastian Netz, 1753, intestate

Lancaster County Orphans Court Proceedings dated 5 Oct 1755:
Estate of SEBASTIAN NETZ, decd. (page 29)
Administrator Michael Netz produces an account of which the balance is approved by the court. The balance is to be distribution to the widow and children according to law; viz.: Margaret (the widow), and children: the said Michael Netz (the eldest son), Sebastian Netz, Margaret Netz, Barbara Netz, and Catharine Netz

For consideration:

Lancaster(Trinity) Lutheran KB, Lancaster County, Pennsylvania:

Married 20 Dec 1739: Joh. George Schonteler and Margaretha Nessin

I have not been able to place the Margaretha Nessin above. I would like to look at the original church record to ensure her surname is not *Neffin*.

Johannes Seitz

1752 Rawley

Johannes Seitz and his brother-in-law Georg Braun (q.v.) signed next to each other on the passenger list of the 1752 ship *Rawley*. Johannes Seitz's wife Margaretha was the daughter of Leonhard Albert. Several of Leonhard's son—Wilhelm Albert (q.v.) and Peter Albert (q.v.)—also went to America.

GERMAN RECORDS:

Russheim Evangelisch KB:

Married 12 Jan 1714: Martin Seitz and Anna Catharina Wentzin (?)

Martin Seitz & his wife Catharina, nee Wenzin, had baptized:
1. Anna Margaretha, born 24 Jan 1717, baptized 25 Jan 1717
2. Johannes, born 30 Sep 1719
3. Maria Barbara, born 20 May 1722, baptized the same day
4. Johann Jacob, born 27 Dec 1724
5. Johann Georg, born 3 Apr 1728

Married --- Dec 1750 (day darkened on microfilm): Johann Jacob Seiz, son of Martin Seiz, and Anna Catharina Heinzin, daughter of Jacob Heinz of Spöck

Married _____ 1740: Georg Braun and Margaretha Seitzin, daughter of Martin Seitz (Note: The microfilmed image is too dark to read the date.)

Married 7 Feb 1747: Johannes Seitz, citizen and tailor, son of Martin Seitz, and Margaretha Albertin, daughter of Leonhart Albert. They had baptized:
1. Catharina Elisabetha, born 14 Dec 1747
2. Catharina Barbara, born 5 Mar 1750
3. Christina, born 25 Oct 1751 (Pastor's notation: "went to the new land")

Below" The baptismal record of Christina Seitz. Note the pastor made note of her parents' emigration next to the word "Eltern" (parents).

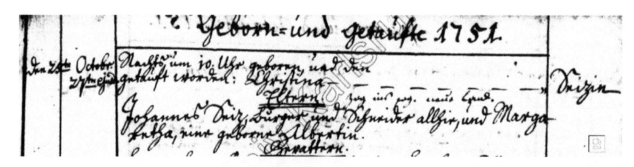

Landeskirchliches Archiv Karlsruhe > Rußheim > Mischbuch 1738 - 1777, Apr. 1800, 1817 - Bild 30 (Accessed via Archion.de)

IMMIGRATION:

Hacker, *Auswanderung aus Baden und dem Breisgau:*

Hacker Emigrant 8408:
Johann Seitz of Russheim, with wife and three children will go to Pennsylvania. Manumitted 21 March 1752.

Ship *Rawley*, qualified 23 Oct 1752 at Philadelphia:

Hans Jerg Steidinger
Johan Philip (X) Frech
George (X) Brown
Johannes Seitz
Lorentz (X) Houshalter
Joseph Burgstahler
Christoph Hacker
Michel Lang
Matheas (X) Miller
Hans Jorg Mock
Hans Jorg Wächter
--All signed next to each other.

PENNSYLVANIA RECORDS:

Reading Lutheran KB, Reading, Berks County, Pennsylvania, USA:

Johannes Seitz & his wife Margaretha had baptized:
1. Jacob, born July 1763, baptized --- 1763, sp. Conrad Kerezinger & Eva Wittington
2. Johann Heinrich, born 20 May 1767, baptized 14 June 1767

Margaretha Seitz, daughter of Johannes & Margaretha Seitz, died 8 Feb 1755, born 1754

Johannes Seitz & his wife Maria Margaret sponsored child of Johann Georg Eckhard & his wife Susanna Barbara in 1760 (child born 11 Feb 1760)

Johannes Seitz & his wife Maria Margaret sponsored child of Jacob Miller & his wife Maria Agatha on 11 Mar 1764

George Seitz & his wife Catharina had baptized:
1. Maria, born 29 Oct 1785, baptized 27 Nov 1785, sp. Johannes Lehmann & his wife Rosina
2. Rosina, born 16 Mar 1788, baptized 11 May 1788, sp. Johannes Lehmann & his wife Rosina
3. Hannah, born 20 Sep 1790, baptized 19 Dec 1790, sp. Johannes Burckhardt & his wife Barbara
4. Veronica, born 10 Jan 1793, baptized 20 Jan 1793, sp. Maderi (midwife)
5. Jacob, born 10 May 1795, baptized 14 June 1795, sp. Jacob Lehman, baker, & his wife Rosina

Berks County, Pennsylvania, Deed Records:

Berks Deed 5-145, dated 20 Dec 1762: Casper Egle to John Seitz, 68 ½ A. Bern Township
Berks Deed 5-148, dated 15 May 1766: John Seitz & his wife Margaret to Michael Miller, 68 ½ A. Bern Township

Berks County, Pennsylvania, Estate Files:

John Seitz, 1780, Reading.
1. Administration Bond dated 23 Oct 1780 granted to George Seitz, the eldest son of John Seitz, deceased, late of the town of Reading.
2. Document dated 23 Oct 1780: Catharina, the widow of John Seitz, relinquishes her right to administer her late husband's estate in favor of George Seitz, the eldest son of the said deceased.

For Further Research:

After the death of his wife Margaret, John Seitz allegedly married Catharina (Sohns) Schneider, the widow of Jacob Schneider (marriage dated 2 May 1780). I have not found evidence of this marriage; however, descendants cite a document dated 7 Aug 1780 signed by "Catharina, the widow of Jacob Schneider, now wife of John Seitz," (see the Berks County Jacob Schneider estate file). By 14 Apr 1781, she signed a document as Catharina Klein. By then, she was allegedly the wife of Michael Klein. Of note: Catharina's mother was allegedly Barbara Kern, daughter of Jacob Kern, who was born in Eggenstein, a village a short distance from Russheim.

Barbara Schmidt (Widow of Friedrich Schmidt)

1749 Ann

Emigration records confirm that the widow Barbara Schmidt married Wendel Keller of Liedolsheim and went to America. Concern was raise in the village of Russheim about her married to Keller and the inheritance that should come to her children (see the section on the Elser family—similar concerns were raised about the marriage of the widow Elser to Henrich Mock of Graben).

Wendel Keller can be found in Pennsylvania records. He was a widower shortly after arrival. I could not locate evidence of the widow Schmidt's children by her former husband. Their son Casper would have been too young to appear on the passenger list of the Ship Ann, and the names of female passengers were not recorded. Genealogists searching for a Casper Schmidt, born circa 1734, may wish to consider this family.

GERMAN RECORDS:

Russheim Evangelisch KB:

Lorentz Speck & his wife Anna Maria had baptized:
1. Maria Barbara, born 2 Jan 1702

Married 24 Nov 1722: Johann Friederich Schmidt, son of Bernhard Schmidt, and Anna Barbara Spöckin, daughter of Lorenz Spöck

Friederich Schmidt & his wife Maria Barbara, born Spöck, had baptized:
1. Christina, born 5 Aug 1726, baptized 6 Aug 1726, sp. Adam Schmidt
2. (Child—microfilm obscured), born --- Jan 1729
3. Catharina Barbara, born 16 July 1731,
4. Casper, born 17 Mar 1734, baptized 18 Mar 1734
5. Maria Margaretha, born 26 Feb 1737, baptized 27 Feb 1737

Died 12 Mar 1747: Friedrich Schmidt (his age is obscured on the microfilm image)

Married 22 Apr 1749: Wendel Keller and Barbara Schmidt, the widow of Friederich Schmidt

IMMIGRATION:

Hacker, *Auswanderungen aus Baden und dem Breisgau.*

Emigrant 9652: Barbara Schmidt, born Speck, widowed Schmidt, of Russheim, with her next husband (not named) of Liedolsheim, went to America. "Kdr im Land bleibt." ("Children remain in the country.")

Ship *Ann*, qualified 28 Sep 1749 at Philadelphia:

Johanes Strauwman
Jacob Landgraff
Johann Friedrich Zimmerman
H. Michael Zimmerman
Johanis Zimmerman
Thomas ( ) Lubek, sick
Wendel (WK) Keller

AMERICAN COLONIAL RECORDS:

Please see the section on Wendel Keller (q.v. I could locate no evidence of his wife **Barbara** or her children surnamed Schmidt.

Martin Schmidt

1737

1737 Rußheim emigrant Martin Schmidt has not been located in American colonial records. His son Johann Georg's 1744 marriage record indicates that his father was in Pennsylvania—or at least had left for Pennsylvania.

GERMAN RECORDS:

Russheim Evangelisch KB:

Married 4 Oct 1708: Martin Schmidt, son of Martin Schmidt, and Jacobina, daughter of Paul Hager

Johann Martin Schmidt & his wife Jacobina had baptized:
1. Maria Margaretha, born 19 Aug 1709, baptized 21 Aug 1709
2. Maria Catharina, born 10 Dec 1711
3. Anna Barbara, born 14 Nov 1713
4. Johann Georg, born 11 Feb 1715, baptized 12 Feb 1715—died 10 May 1794
5. Johannes, born 1 Nov 1716 (day of birth difficult to read)—died 21 Aug 1717
6. Hans Michael, born 27 June 1718, baptized 29 June 1718
7. Elisabetha, born 27 Jan 1720, baptized 29 Jan 1720
8. Johann Friederich, born 10 Aug 1724
9. Lorenz, born 23 Jan 1727

Married 10 November 1744: Johann Georg Schmidt, son of Martin Schmidt who went to Pennsylvania (see image below) and Anna Catharina, daughter of Michael Löhlin, of Russheim. They had baptized:
1. Johann Georg, baptized 6 Aug 1745 (cross next to child's name; father a resident of Russheim)
2. Johannes, baptized 20 June 1747—died 22 Feb 1788
3. Johann Michael, baptized 3 July 1749 (cross next to child's name)

Note: Son Georg Schmidt remained in Russheim until his death in 1794. His family was not fully researched.

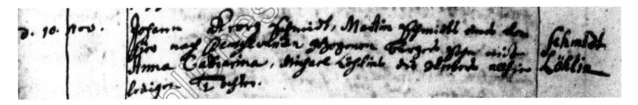

Landeskirchliches Archiv Karlsruhe > Rußheim > Mischbuch 1738 - 1777, Apr. 1800, 1817 - Bild 238 (Accessed via Archion.de)

IMMIGRATION:

Hacker,, *Auswanderungen aus Baden und dem Breisgau*.

Hacker Emigrant File 9125:
Martin Schmidt of Russheim, filed October 1737, netto 540 florins. Destination not indicated.

Hacker Emigrant File 9129:
Joh. Georg Schmidt of Russheim, the eldest son of Mtns. (Martinus?), with wife and 5 children, with father. Filed 12 Nov 1737. Remained in the country, 10 May 1738.

As shown previously, Georg Schmidt's 1744 marriage record indicates that his father Martin had gone to Pennsylvania. I find no evidence of Martin Schmidt in passenger arrivals list for 1737-1738. I would expect him to be aboard the Ship *William* with other Russheimers who emigrated that year; however, the only Schmidt on the passenger list is Mathias Schmidt who came from nearby Spöck.

A Martin Schmidt did arrive in 1742.

In regards to Hacker Emigrant 9129: I presume that the "wife and five children" refer to father Martin Schmidt, his wife, and five children. I find no evidence of Martin Schmidt's other children in Russheim records. Presumably they left with their father.

AMERICAN COLONIAL RECORDS:

I could not locate evidence of a Martin Schmidt with a wife named Jacobina in the American colonies.

Johann Adam Speck and Bernhard Speck

1752 Phoenix (Johann Adam Speck)
1754 Henrietta (Bernhard Speck)

Brothers Adam Speck and Bernhard Speck emigrated separately but reunited in Pennsylvania. Bernhard's Pennsylvania marriage record identifies Russheim as his native German village.

GERMAN RECORDS:

Russheim Evangelisch KB:

Married 6 Nov 1714: Hans Adam Spock, widower, and Anna Catharina, daughter of Diebolt Jockin

Hans Adam Spöck & his wife Maria Catharina, born Jockin, had baptized:
1. Johann Adam, born 6 July 1717, baptized 7 July 1717
2. Hans Georg, born 8 May 1719, baptized 11 May 1719 (cross next to name)
3. Maria Catharina, born 18 Feb 1722, baptized 19 Feb 1722—died 3 Sep 1804
4. Apollonia, born 10 Jan 1724, baptized 12 Jan 1724
5. Maria Barbara, baptized 2 Mar 1725—died 13 Sep 1733
6. Bernhard, born 28 Aug 1726
7. Martin, born 22 Mar 1730 (cross next to name)

--Another child—Johann Michael--may have been born to this couple in the fall of 1720 (entry difficult to read).

Married 12 Jan 1740: Adam Spock, citizen and shoemaker, son of Adam Spock, and Anna Barbara Spock, daughter of Martin Spock.

They had baptized:
1. Catharina Barbara, baptized 24 Nov 1742
2. Johann Adam, born 12 Aug 1747—died 13 Feb 1749
3. Frederica Christina, born 4 Mar 1751 (pastor's notation: "went to the new land")

Above: On1the 1751 baptismal record for Friderica Christina Spock, daughter of Adam Spock and Barbara Spock, the pastor wrote that the family went to the New Land (neue land). Source: Landeskirchliches Archiv Karlsruhe > Rußheim > Mischbuch 1738 - 1777,Apr. 1800,1817 - Bild 29(Accessed via Archion.de)

Hacker, *Auswanderungen aus Baden und dem Breisgau.*

Emigrant 9653: Johann (-Adam) Speck, Russheim, mit Fr, 2 Ki, Vm 25.30; Mm. 7 Mar 1752.

Ship *Phoenix*, qualified 22 Nov 1752 at Philadelphia:

<u>Johann Adam Speck (signed his name)</u>
Johann Georg Jeck (signed his name)
--Signed next to each other.

Note: Johann Adam Speck's mother was Catharina Jock, daughter of Diebold Jock. The Johann Georg *Jeck* signing next to him on the passenger list may be a relation.

Ship *Henrietta*, qualified 22 Oct 1754 at Philadelphia:

Bernhard Speck

PENNNSYLVANIA RECORDS:

Warwick Lutheran KB, Lancaster County, Pennsylvania:

(complete surname to 1799)

Johann Adam Speck had baptized:
1. Eva, born 12 Aug 1755, baptized 20 Sep 1755, sp. Bernhardt Speck & Eva Braunen
2. Johannes, born 28 June 1758, baptized 20 Sep 1758, sp. Bernhart Speck & his wife Magdalena
3. Johannes, born 2 June 1765, baptized 1 Trinity 1765, sp. Johannes Schad & his wife

Adam Spek & his wife sponsored child of Marcus Jams on Sexagesima 1766

Lancaster Lutheran KB, Lancaster County, Pennsylvania:

Joh. Bernhart Spöck from Russheim in Durlach married 19 Apr 1757 Magdalena Grözingen from Rotenacker

Bernhard Spöck & his wife Magdalena had baptized:
1. Barbara, born 1 Nov 1759, baptized 11 Nov 1759, sp. Johannes Koch & his wife Barbara

St. Luke's Lutheran KB, Schaefferstown, Lebanon County, Pennsylvania:

Died (buried?) 16 Apr 1773 in Heidelberg: Adam Speck, aged 63 years

Martin Speck (or Spöck)

1738 Friendship

Upon arrival at Philadelphia, Martin Speck signed his name next to his brother-in-law Friederich Hahnle of Graben.

GERMAN RECORDS:

Russheim Evangelisch KB:

Hans Martin Speckh & his wife Anna Catharina had baptized:
1. Hans Martin, born 5 Oct 1698, baptized 9 Oct 1698

Married 10 Oct 1731: Martin Speck, son of Johann Martin Speck, and Susanna Hainlin, daughter of Johann Michael Hainlin of Graben

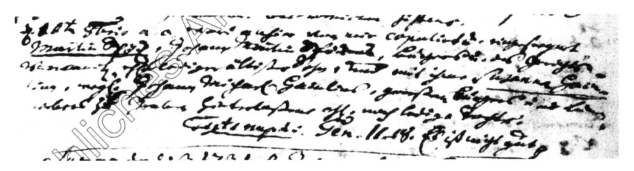

Landeskirchliches Archiv Karlsruhe > Rußheim > Mischbuch 1692 - 1738 - Bild 64 (Accessed via Archion.de)

Martin Spöck & his wife Susanna had baptized:
1. Margaretha, born 29 July 1732, baptized 31 July 1732 (cross next to name)
2. Christian Barbara, born 20 Feb 1734, baptized 21 Feb 1734—died 27 Jan 1737
3. Susanna, born 16 Mar 1736, baptized 17 Mar 1736—died 27 July 1736
4. Adam, born 7 (?) July 1737

IMMIGRATION:

Hacker, *Auswanderungen aus Baden und dem Breisgau.*

Emigrant 9650: Martin Speck, Russheim, 277 fl.; Mm October 1737. 20 Sep 1738.

Ship *Friendship*, qualified 20 Sep 1738 at Philadelphia:

Johan Martin Karcher, age 19
Daniel Friedrich Reinekh, age 32
Hans Enger (X) Bough, age 40 (Hans Jurg Buck on List A)
Dedrich (FH) Hilie, age 20 (Fredrich Haylie on List A—probably <u>Fredrich</u> Hahnle/Hainle)
<u>Martin (+) Speck, age 35</u>
Hans Georg Konig, age 30
Johan Wendel Braun, age 37

PENNSYLVANIA RECORDS:

Stoever, Rev. John Casper, personal register:

Martin Speck (Swatara Congregation) had baptized:
1. Anna Maria, born 15 Jan 1741, baptized 16 Apr 1742, sp. Sigmund Haehnle, Jr., & Anna Maria Becker
2. Martin, born 23 Mar 1744, baptized 15 Apr 1744, sp. Frederick Haehnle & his wife
3. Eleanora, born 30 Mar 1746, baptized 27 Apr 1746, sp. Bernhardt Friedle & his wife
4. Maria Catharina, born 28 Aug 1748, baptized 4 Sep 1748, sp. Sigmund Haehnle & his wife
5. Johann Michael, born 29 Dec 1750, baptized 21 Jan 1751, sp. Michael Kleber & his wife Elisabeth
6. Johann Jacob, born 29 Apr 1753, baptized 20 May 1753, sp. Michael Kleber & his wife Elisabeth
7. Johannes, born 18 Sep 1754, baptized 7 Oct 1754, sp. Jacob Loresch & his wife

Martin Speck & his wife sponsored child of Antonius Rosenbaum on 16 Apr 1742 (Swatara)
Martin Speck & his wife sponsored child of Bernhardt Friedel on 23 May 1743 (Swatara)

Martin Speck & his wife Susanna sponsored child of Michael Kleber on 19 Mar 1749 (Swatara)

Leonhardt Fischer & Margaretha Speck sponsored child of George Michael Wildtfang on 27 Oct 1751 (Tulpehocken)

Daniel Born & Margaretha Speck sponsored children of David Dreher and Jacob Dreisch & his wife Susanna on 12 Apr 1752 (Lebanon) [two separate baptisms on the same day]

Conrad Roenninger & Margaretha Speck sponsored child of Johannes Haeffele on 17 Feb 1752 (Swatara)

Friederich Werner

Professor Werner Hacker did not identify an emigrant surnamed Werner from Russheim; however, Clifford Neal Smith in *Emigrants from the West-German Fuerstenberg Territories (Baden and the Palatinate) to America and Central Europe, 1712, 1737, 1787* includes the following:

Friedrich Werner of Russheim, manumitted 1737. Intends to go to America.

GERMAN RECORDS:

Russheim Evangelisch KB:

Caspar Werner & his wife Catharina had baptized:
1. Hans Friedrich, born 8 Sep 1699, baptized 10 Sep 1699

Married 11 Jan 1723: Johann Friederich Werner, son of Casper Werner, and Catharina Rothin, daughter of --- Roth

Friedrich Werner & his wife Catharina had baptized:
1. Catharina Barbara, born 30 Sep 1728
2. Margaretha, born 2 Sep 1733, baptized 3 Sep 1733

Note: A child Maria Catharina Werner born to Friederich Werner and wife Maria Barbara on 19 June 1729.

--No further record of this family in the Russheim records.

IMMIGRATION:

I did not locate a person of this name in the 1737-1739 timeframe in Strassburger and Hinke's *Pennsylvania German Pioneers*. Perhaps this emigrant did not travel to Pennsylvania. It is also possible that he was a victim of the Year of the Destroying Angel in 1738.

AMERICAN COLONIAL RECORDS:

I was unable to locate a person in America who fit this emigrant's profile. A Casper Werner (often Verner) was taxed in early Warwick Township, Lancaster County, Pennsylvania—an area where many Baden-Durlach emigrants settled.

Catharina Zimmerman and her sons Johann Friederich, Johann Michael, and Johannes Zimmerman

1749 Ann

GERMAN RECORDS:

Russheim Evangelisch KB:

Married 13 Apr 1723: Johann Michael Zimmerman, son of Johann Michael Zimmerman, and Anna Catharina Hagerin, daughter of Sebastian Hager.

Michael Zimmerman & his wife Anna Catharina, born Hagerin, had baptized:
1. Johann Friedrich, born 7 Feb 1724
2. Johann Michael, born 1 May 1725
3. Johannes, born 18 Feb 1727
4. Maria Catharina, born 22 Jan 1729
5. Elisabetha, born 17 Oct 1733, baptized 18 Oct 1733

"Ex illegitimo concubitu"
Johann Michael Zimmerman and Sabina ____ (?) had baptized:
1. Johannes, born 16 Aug 1731 –died 20 May 1735

Died 6 Jan 1742: Michael Zimmerman, son of Michael Zimmerman & Margaretha Hoblerin (?) age 54 years

IMMIGRATION:

Hacker, *Auswanderung aus Baden und dem Breisgau:*

Hacker Emigrant 11380:
Catharine Zimmerman, a widow, born Hager, of Russheim. Her children are grown. Will go to Pennsylvania. Manumitted 1 February 1749.

Hacker Emigrant 3385:
Catharine Hager, the wife of Zimmerman, Russheim, *deren Kinder erwachsen sind* (her children are grown). Will go to Pennsylvania. Manumitted 1 February 1749.

Ship *Ann*, qualified 28 Sep 1749 at Philadelphia:

Johannes Weber
Johanes Strauwman
Jacob Landgraff
Johann Friedrich Zimmerman
H. Michael Zimmerman
Johanis Zimmerman
Thomas ( ) Lubek, sick
Wendel (WK) Keller
….
Hans Adam Nees
Hans Nes

PENNSYLVANIA RECORDS:

Stoever, Rev. John Casper, personal register:

Johann Friederich Zimmerman married 23 Oct 1750 Maria Margaretha Lutz (Warwick Congregation)

Warwick Lutheran KB, Lancaster County, Pennsylvania:

Joh. Friederich Zimmerman had baptized:
1. Joh. Friederich, born 1 Sep 1751, baptized 8 Sep 1751, sp. Martin Spickler & his wife
2. Joh. Michael, born 21 Aug 1752, baptized 23 Aug 1752, sp. Joh. Nicholas Schmidt and Catharina Zimmermanin
3. Eva Catharina, born 7 Mar 1754, baptized 10 Mar 1754, sp. Jo. Lutz and Catharina Zimmermannin
4. Johannes, born 3 Jan 1756, sp. Conrad Kerlinger & Barbara Weidmanin
5. Margaretha, born 24 Jan 1759, sp. Matteis Cammerer & Margaretha Nehsin
6. Joh. Adam, born 27 Dec 1760, sp. Joh. Adam Nehs & Margaretha Oberlin
7. Martin, born 11 Dec 1762, sp. Martin Spikler & his wife
8. Joh. Leonhard, born 20 June 1764, sp. Leonhard Miller & Eva Nesin
9. Maria Elisabetha, born 20 Feb 1766, baptized Judicate 1766, sp. Johannes Zimmerman Maria Nesin

Friederich Zimmermann & his wife Margaretha sponsored child of Martin Spickler on 24 Feb 1751

Bindnagel's Lutheran KB, Lebanon County, Pennsylvania:

John Michael Zimmerman, born 1 May 1725, died March 1805, aged 79 years, 11 months. Born in Baden-Durlach. His parents were named Michael and Mary. He came to this country in his 25th year. He married Eva Koenig on 15 May 1750. (Eva Koenig was a stepdaughter of J. Geo. Beyer.) Begat 8 children—3 sons and 2 daughters survive.

Other Russheim Emigrants Identified by Hacker

I investigated the following emigrants identified by Hacker but determined that it is unlikely that they went to America.

Lorentz Roth

Hacker, *Auswanderung aus Baden und dem Breisgau:*

Hacker Emigrant 8168:
Lorenz Roth of Russheim. Manumitted 10 October 1768. Destination not given.

Lorenz Roth & his wife Maria Eva had baptized:
1. Lorentz, born 22 Feb 1743

--Not found in Strassburger and Hinke. No evidence of migration to America.

Michael Weber

Hacker, *Auswanderung aus Baden und dem Breisgau:*

Hacker Emigrant 10768:
Michael Weber, citizen of Russheim, will go to Pennsylvania. Manumitted 13 February 1737.

--Note: In Clifford Neal Smith's abstract of this emigrant file he adds that "he may not have emigrated." The Russheim Evangelisch records below suggest that the Michael Weber family remained in Russheim. I see no other person of that name who may have left for Pennsylvania in 1737.

Johann Weber & his wife Anna Catharina had baptized:
1. Joh. Michael, born 7 Apr 1709, baptized 9 Apr 1709

Married 8 June 1732: Johann Michael Weber, son of Johann Weber, and Rosina Hornerin, daughter of Michael Hörner

Hans Michael Weber & his wife Rosina had baptized:
1. Johannes, born 4 Dec 1732, baptized 5 Dec 1732--died 20 Jan 1734
2. Johann Michael, born 23 May 1735, baptized 24 May 1735--died 30 Mar 1735
3. Johann Christoph, born 6 Apr 1746, baptized 9 Apr 1746—died 18 Feb 1750

Married 25 Jan 1745: Joseph Burgstahler, widower, and Rosina Weberin, widow.

Joseph Burgstahler & his wife Rosina Hornerin had baptized:
1. Christina, born 4 July 1747, baptized 4 July 1747

Burkhard Weber

Hacker, *Auswanderung aus Baden und dem Breisgau:*

Hacker Emigrant 10789:
Burkhard Weber of Russheim. Manumitted 28 August 1755. Destination not given.

--Note: I did not locate anyone of this name in the Russheim Evangelisch records. I also did not find this name in Strassburger and Hinke's Pennsylvania German Pioneers.

Recommended Resources

Genwiki

This German website links each German community to related historical and genealogical resources. (Main page: http://wiki-de.genealogy.net/Hauptseite) It is written in German but online translators can assist.

Dettenheim (Baden)
http://wiki-de.genealogy.net/GOV:LIEEIM_W7521

Ortssippenbucher

Ortssippenbuchs are village lineage books. For more than a century, German genealogists have created ortssippenbuchs. They often serve as a short cut in the research process. The compilers use local church record to group family units. Often, all entries in the local church books are used to create the ortsippenbuch.

The following ortsippenbuch has been created for Russheim:

Lang, Wilhelm Ludwig, *Rußheimer Familien Ortissippenbuch 1692 bis 1920* (Dettenheim, Germany : Gemeinde Dettenheim, 2003) 784 pages. ISBN: 3-00-008164-X

Copies of this book—and other Baden ortssippenbuchs—can be purchased online.

Local History

The following history of Russheim, written in 1860, is available:

Fritz Hoeck: *Geschichte des Pfarrdorfes Rußheim bei Karlsruhe mit Berücksichtigung der Umgegend. Ein kleiner Beitrag zur vaterländischen Geschichte.* Braun, Karlsruhe 1860.

This work is out-of-copyright and can be found in several digital repositories.

Digital text available for free via Google Play:
https://play.google.com/store/books/details?id=uqNYAAAAcAAJ&hl=en

1709 Heads of Household of Russheim in Baden-Durlach

In 1709, a list of the heads of households for Baden-Durlach was compiled. In 1936, Jacob Hermann of Karlsruhe published the list.

Original source: Jacob Hermann. Einwohnerbuch der Markgrafschaft Baden-Durlach im Jahre 1709. Schopfheim (Baden), 1936.

Transcriptions can be found online.

Click here to access the transcriptions of neighboring villages:
http://wiki-de.genealogy.net/Kategorie:Einwohnerbuch_Baden-Durlach_1709

Einwohnerliste Russheim von 1709

Quelle: *Einwohnerbuch der Markgrafschaft Baden-Durlach 1709* von Hermann Jacob.

Beyer, Hans Bernhard
Boltz, Jakob
Boltz, Wendel
Braun, hans
Elßer, Hans Martin, der Schleifmüller
Geiß, Veit
Gangwolf, Hans Michael
Haaß, Wendel
Hackher, Georg
Hager, Friedrich
Hager, Peter
Hännßler, Hans Andreas
Haußhalt, Hans Michael, Anwalt
Karch, Hans
Karch, Lorenz`ens Wittib
Kerber, Georg
Kerber, Peter
Kuhn, Ulrich
Moß, Jakob
Neeß, Hans Adam
Neeß, Hans Michael
Neeß, Sebastian
Reinacher, Jakob
Reinacher, Sebastian
Roth, Hans
Roth, Hans Paul
Roth, Michael, der Schultheiß
Schmidt, Daniel
Schmidt, Georg
Schmidt, Jakob
Schmidt, Lorenz

Siegel, Bernhard
Siegel, Peter
Speckh, Christoph
Speckh, Christoph`s Wittib
Speckh, Hans Martin
Speckh, Lorenz
Stirn, Hans Michael
Stutz, Christoph
Weber, Adam
Weber, Hans
Weickh, hans Jakob
Wörner, Georg
Wörner, Hans
Wörner, Hans Michael`s Wittib
Wörner, Jakob
Wörner, Kaspar
Wörner, Sebastian`s Wittib
Zimmermann, Hans Michael
Zweckher, Hans Michael

Addendum: Russheim Hager Family

Hager

I could not document any persons surnamed Hager who left this village for America; however, a number of female Hagers married men who did emigrate. Here follows information compiled on the early Hager families of Russheim:

Russheim Evangelisch KB:

Hans Michael Hager, son of Paul Hager, married 17 May 1718 Anna Catharina Spöck, daughter of Paul Spöck. They had baptized:
1. Hans Michael, born 20 Aug 1719, baptized 22 Aug 1719
2. Johannes, born 21 Sep 1720, baptized 22 Sep 1720
3. Hans Adam, born 5 May 1723, baptized 5 May 1723
4. Johann Georg, born 5 Jan 1726, baptized 7 Jan 1726
5. Johann Friedrich, born 4 Jan 1729

Hans Sebastian Hager, son of Johann Sebastian Hager, married 15 June 1697 Anna Catharina Haushalter, daughter of Johannes Haushalter. They had baptized:
1. Johann Michael, born 2 Feb 1697
2. Maria Margaretha, born 16 July 1698
3. Maria Catharina, born 23 Nov 1699
4. Maria Barbara, born 2 Sep 1702
5. Anna Christina, born 25 Apr 1704
6. Johann Martin, born 20 July 1707
7. Anna Elisabetha, born 19 Mar 1709

Maria Barbara Buchin married 20 Jan 1722 Johann Michael Haushalter, son of Lorentz Haushalter (?—confusing entry—Maria Barbara Hagerin also mentioned.

Johann Michael Hager, son of Hans Sebastian Hager, married 19 Nov 1719 Maria Barbara Haushalter, daughter of Michael Haushalter. They had baptized:
1. Johann Michael, born 27 Apr 1722, baptized 27 Apr 1722
2. Johannes, born 8 May 1725, baptized 10 May 1725
3. Johann Frederich, born 23 Mar 1728, baptized 23 Mar 1728
4. Johann Peter, born 18 Feb 1731, baptized 19 Feb 1731
5. Johann Georg, born --- 1733

Married 13 Apr 1723: Johann Michael Zimmerman, son of Johann Michael Zimmerman, and Anna Catharina Hagerin, daughter of Sebastian Hager

Johann Michael Neess & his wife Elisabetha, nee Hagerin, had baptized:
1. Joh. Georg, baptized 11 Jan 1731 (cross next to name)--died 5 July 1734

2. Maria Barbara, baptized 3 Apr 1733
3. Johann Michael, baptized 2 Oct 1734
4. Hans Georg, baptized 10 Oct 1736

Married 9 Dec 1726: Hans Adam Elsser, widower, and Margaretha Hagerin

Notes on Sources

Commonly Used Abbreviations:

Adm. = administrated by
b. = born
bp. = baptized
c. = circa (about)
Ex./Exrs. = executors
e.g. = such as
i.e. = that is
KB = Kirchenbuch (church book)
m. = married
Nat. = naturalized
q.v. = which see (another immigrant in the text)
Sp. = sponsored by
Twp. = township
Wit. = witness(es)

IMMIGRATION RECORDS

Ship Passengers List Arriving at the Port of Philadelphia

All ship passenger lists are taken from Strassburger and Hinke's *Pennsylvania German Pioneers*:

> Ralph Beaver Strassburger and William John Hinke. *Pennsylvania German Pioneers: A Publication of the Original Lists of Arrivals in the Port of Philadelphia from 1727 to 1808* (Three Volume Set). Picton Press. Camden, Maine: 1992.

Beginning in 1727, captains of ships arriving at the Port of Philadelphia carrying had to provide a list of the foreign passengers on board the ship. Typically, only male passengers aged 16 and upwards were compiled—however, some early lists include women and children. (Generally only children aged 5 years and upwards would be noted. They were chargeable freight. Those under 5 were transported free of charge.)

In Strassburger and Hinke, the captain's list was called List A. Two additional lists exist—one called List B and the other List C. Important: A member of the crew generally compiled List A, but male passengers aged 16 and upwards signed Lists B and C. Passengers signed List B and List C before a member of the Philadelphia court, typically at the Court House of Philadelphia. In signing List B, the immigrants disavowed their former rulers. In signing List C, immigrants acknowledged English's King George II as their rightful ruler. List C exists for all ships arriving at Philadelphia from 1729 to 1775. For some ships all three lists survive, for others, only List C. The date of qualification is the date that the document was signed at the court house in Philadelphia.

Important: Not every person on List A appears on Lists B and C. Lists B and C were signed at the same moment in time. The immigrant walked from one desk where he signed List B to another desk where he signed List C. But List A may have been taken earlier. I find the order of names to be the same, but it is common for List A to include names not on the other lists. The primary reason: Illness. Imagine the captain or crew member compiling List A as passengers prepared to disembark the ship to walk to the court house: A passenger too ill to make the trip would appear on List A but not on List B or List C. A person in this circumstance would later need to apply for naturalization in order to enjoy the full rights of citizenship.

In 1992, Picton Press published a deluxe three volume edition of *Pennsylvania German Pioneers*, For Volume 2, Picton included images of the original List C's—allowing researchers to look at original signatures. This volume is important for a number of reasons, among them:
1. Interpreting signatures is an art form. Some transcriptions are incorrect—with the full blame on the often incomprehensible scrawl of the German writer.
2. Signatures can be compared to signatures in other American records—helping to identify when a person arrived at Philadelphia.

In my work, I include the name of the immigrant as well as surrounding names. Why? They came in groups. People grouped with those familiar to them. In my research monographs, I find time and time again that a person signed his name to Lists B and C next to others who came from the same European village.

Naturalization Records

Colonial immigrants who signed List C (see above) at the Philadelphia Court House swore allegiance to the British Crown. At that moment, they essentially enjoyed the rights of British citizenship. Young immigrant men under the age of 16—who could not legally take the oaths—were still considered foreign nationals. Legally, they would need to apply for citizenship in order to enjoy the full rights of citizenship. This process was called naturalization.

Men unable or unwilling to sign the oaths upon arrival would also need to become naturalized citizens if they wished to transfer real estate to other persons.

A person who appears in colonial naturalization records was born in a foreign county (i.e., non-British). However, I have found individuals who took the required oaths for citizenship upon arrival yet also obtained naturalization. In such cases it seems reasonable to conclude that the person needed proof or evidence that they were a British subject. Perhaps documentation attesting to such had been lost or destroyed.

When searching for naturalization, I begin with Lloyd Bockstruck's *Denizations and Naturalizations in the British Colonies in America, 1607-1775*. In this work, Mr. Bockstruck compiled naturalizations from all American colonies, organizing them alphabetically, including the date and location of naturalization. This work effectively synthesis early naturalizations from New York, New Jersey, Maryland, Virginia, and Pennsylvania—the locations of settlement for most people that passed through the Port of Philadelphia.

This book can currently be accessed with a subscription to Ancestry.com:

Ancestry.com. *Denizations and Naturalizations in the British Colonies in America, 1607-1775* [database on-line]. Provo, UT, USA: Ancestry.com Operations Inc, 2006.

Original data: Bockstruck, Lloyd DeWitt. *Denizations and Naturalizations in the British Colonies in America, 1607-1775*. Baltimore, MD, USA: Genealogical Publishing Co., 2005.

The *Pennsylvania Archives, Second Series: Volume II* includes all naturalizations taking place in Pennsylvania from 1740 to 1773. This publication is out of copyright and can easily be found online.

CHURCH RECORDS

I include a short reference to the parish records in which the records were found: Name of the church and location of the church.

Over the centuries, the names of many churches have changed. In such instances, I typically use the name of the local community. For example: In Lancaster, Lancaster County, Pennsylvania, the Lutheran church's official name is The Evangelical Lutheran Church of the Holy Trinity. In my research, I simply refer to this church as "Lancaster Lutheran."

A problem with citing locations is that names and divisions have changed over time. To help locate the church, I cite the modern day location by county. For example: Dauphin County was formed out of Lancaster County, Pennsylvania, in 1785. Prior to 1785, all townships in Dauphin County were part of Lancaster County—thus, persons born in those townships prior to division were natives of Lancaster County, Pennsylvania, even though they were born in modern day Dauphin County. For those who look at my database, I choose to cite the birth location as it were at the actual time of birth.

Whenever I cite information from a church record, I am affirming that—with my own eyes—I examined either the original church book or a trusted transcription. Multiple transcriptions exist for some church records. Below, I have compiled the resources that I typically consult.

F. Edward Wright, Pennsylvania Church Records of the Eighteenth Century, Family Line Publications

Mr. Wright compiled transcriptions of scores of early church records that he then published in a series of books. He included records to the year 1800.

1. Adams County, Pennsylvania (one volume)
2. Berks County, Pennsylvania (five volumes)
3. Bucks County, Pennsylvania (four volumes)
4. Chester County, Pennsylvania (three volumes)
5. Cumberland County, Pennsylvania (one volume)
6. Delaware County, Pennsylvania (one volume)
7. Dauphin County, Pennsylvania (one volume)
8. Lancaster County, Pennsylvania (six volumes)

9. Lebanon County, Pennsylvania (one volume)
10. Philadelphia County, Pennsylvania (three volumes)
11. York County, Pennsylvania (three volumes)

Mr. Wright's church record compilations also extend to neighboring states: New Jersey, Maryland, and Delaware.

Important: Mr. Wright did not (or could not) include *all* eighteenth century church records available within a county in his books. In more than a few cases, reliable transcriptions already existed. In the introduction to each volume, he often notes other churches not included, indicating how/where those records might be accessed.

John T. Humphrey Pennsylvania Births Series (Humphrey Publications: Washington, D.C.)

Mr. Humphrey compiled a series of books compiling eighteenth century birth/baptismal records within a Pennsylvania county. Next to each birth/baptism, he cites the church in which the record appears. He works often include churches not appearing in F. Edward Wright's eighteenth century church records series.

His collected works essentially serve as an index to Pennsylvania baptismal records to the year 1800.

Available counties:
1. Berks County (two volumes)
2. Bucks County
3. Carbon County, 1795-1825; Monroe County, 1741-1825; Schuylkill County, 1755-1825 (one volume)
4. Chester County
5. Delaware County
6. Dauphin County, 1757-1825
7. Cumberland County
8. Lancaster County (two volumes)
9. Lebanon County
10. Lehigh County
11. Montgomery County
12. Philadelphia County (three volumes)
13. Schuylkill County
14. York County

Pennsylvania and New Jersey, Church and Town Records, 1669-1999

Ancestry.com. *Pennsylvania and New Jersey, Church and Town Records, 1669-1999* [database on-line]. Lehi, UT, USA: Ancestry.com Operations, Inc., 2011.

Ancestry partnered with the Historical Society of Pennsylvania (HSP) to digitize its collection of church records. Some church records are transcripts, others digitized images.

The HSP's collection is not complete but has hundreds of church records in Pennsylvania, Maryland, and New Jersey available for easy viewing.

Important: Most—but not all—of the records are indexed and searchable.

Pastor Frederick S. Weiser Collection

A passionate genealogist, Pastor Frederick S. Weiser translated numerous eighteenth century German parish registers.

1. Trinity Lutheran Church Records, Lancaster, Pennsylvania, 1730-1812 [four volumes] (This work co-authored with Debra D. Smith.) Published by Closson Press.
2. Records of Pastoral Acts of Trinity Evangelical Lutheran Church, New Holland, Lancaster County, Pennsylvania, 1730-1799. Published by the Pennsylvania German Society, 1977.
3. Records of Pastoral Acts at Emanuel Lutheran Church, known in the eighteenth century as the Warwick congregation, near Brickerville, Elizabeth Township, Lancaster County, Pennsylvania, 1743-1799. Published by the Pennsylvania German Society, 1983.

Archive.org and Google Books

These online databases have hundreds of thousands of digitized books available—including scores of genealogical interest. Search "Tohickon Reformed" or "New Hanover Lutheran" and one can quickly access transcriptions of the early church books that were published in books now out of copyright.

LAND RECORDS

Pennsylvania Propriety and Commonwealth Land Records

Donna Bingham Munger published a definitive book on Pennsylvania land records:

Donna Bingham Munger. *Pennsylvania Land Records: A History and Guide for Research*. Published in cooperation with the Pennsylvania Historical and Museum Commission. Scholarly Resources, Inc.: Wilmington, Delaware (1991).

This book explains the land acquisition process in Colonial Pennsylvania and delineates the available records. A brief version can be found on the Land Records Overview webpage on the Pennsylvania Historical & Museum Commission website.

Three basic steps were needed to acquire land from the Proprietors of Pennsylvania (viz., the Penn family):
1. Application (a request for a warrant)
2. Warrant to Survey (a certificate authorizing a survey of a tract of land; providing a legal claim to specific vacant real estate, including terms of purchase)
3. Survey (hiring a professional surveyor to draw metes and bounds)
4. Return (the surveyor sends—or returns—the survey to the Pennsylvania Land Office)
5. Patent (full payment complete; full legal ownership—a deed from the Penns or the Commonwealth conveying clear title and all rights to a private owner)

Original images of the land warrants are available in the Ancestry.com database *Pennsylvania, Land Warrants and Applications, 1733-1952* [database on-line]. Provo, UT, USA: Ancestry.com Operations, Inc., 2012. This database is searchable.

The PMHC Land Records Overview page includes a number of valuable digitized records:
1. Warrant Registers by County: While the Ancestry Land Warrants database is searchable, I find that some entries found in the warrant registers have been omitted. Warrant Registers are grouped a last name and then by date of warrant. If you know the county in which an ancestor lived, then the warrant register for that county should be inspected.
2. Images of the copied surveys. In the aforesaid warrant registers, reference is given to the location of the survey if it was returned to the Land Office.
3. Patent indexes: The warrant registers include reference to where a patent was recorded (if the land was patented)-but separate online indexes exist grouped alphabetically by the patentee's last name. (The person who took out the warrant is not always the same person who took out the patent.)
4. Township warrantee maps (for some counties): In the twentieth century, government workers created maps by township in which they plotted all the surveys from original warrants. Essentially, these maps recreate the early communities by showing where one claimants land was in relation to other people.

Note: As of summer 2017, images of the original patent records are not available. In most patents recorded prior to the year 1781, the recorder includes the history of all persons who had legal ownership of the tract from the date of the warrant to the date of the patent. Often these embedded histories include transfers not recorded at the county level.

Pennsylvania County Land Records

When land was sold, both parties entered in a legal contract called a deed of assignment. In early Pennsylvania, these land transfers were recorded at the county level.

A number of Pennsylvania counties currently have the old deed records—including indexes—available for viewing. Please visit the Recorder of Deeds webpage for the following counties in order to access and view early lands:
1. Berks County
2. Dauphin County
3. Lancaster County

The LDS church filmed the deed records of most Pennsylvania counties. Search the LDS catalogue to determine what holdings exist. As of summer 2017, Family Search has not made these films available online.

ESTATE RECORDS

Pennsylvania Estate Records

In Pennsylvania, a person either died testate (with a last will and testament) or intestate (without a last will and testament). A person who died testate named executors in his or her last will and testament who then was charged with carrying out the intentions of the deceased. A person who died intestate had their estate administered according to state law. The local court would appoint estate administrators—generally next of kin.

The administrators for those who died without a will often appeared before the Orphans Court of the county of record to address needs and obligations.

Important: Not all persons who died left estates. An elderly person often disposed of his or her estate such that there was no need for later court proceedings. Also, some people left such a small estate that heirs simply "agreed" to what should be done so that the costs of a court settlement could be avoided. It is not uncommon for a person to simply "disappear."

Estates were administered at the county level. These records are largely complete across Pennsylvania. Several databases allow easy access to these records:

"Pennsylvania, Probate Records, 1683-1994." Images. *FamilySearch*. http://FamilySearch.org : accessed 2017. Citing County Courthouses, state-wide, Pennsylvania.

Ancestry.com. *Pennsylvania, Wills and Probate Records, 1683-1993* [database on-line]. Provo, UT, USA: Ancestry.com Operations, Inc., 2015.

Each database includes numerous digitized books pertaining to estates organized by the county level. The holdings vary by county. The Ancestry database is searchable by estate, although not yet fully indexed.

There are some differences between the two collections: A researcher should take care to check the holdings for a particular county in each database.

In my research, when I identify information as coming from estate records or from an estate file, it means that—in the county referenced—I saw a document connected to a specific estate file with that information. If available, I give the book and page in which the information appeared. For example: Lancaster Will B517 means that I found the information in Lancaster County, Pennsylvania, Will Book B, page 517.

Both LDS/Family Search and Ancestry.com have databases that include the same types of records for other states.

Researchers should always check the Register of Wills website for the county in which their ancestors lived. Some counties—such as Berks County, Pennsylvania—have their old estate records available online for viewing.

Decades ago, the Genealogical Society of Pennsylvania (GSP) abstracted the wills of most Pennsylvania counties formed prior to 1820. They abstracts are out of copyright. Most are posted free online. Visit the US Genweb Archives for each Pennsylvania county and look at county archives index.

Warning: Some of these early abstracts were poorly done. I use abstracts to look wills but I always read the original.

TAX RECORDS

Tax registers are an invaluable resource. Generally, taxes were paid yearly at the county level. The following persons were taxable:

1. The head of a household.
2. All men aged 21 years or older.
    a. If the person owned real estate, he was taxed as a freeholder.
    b. IF the person was married but rented his home, then he was taxed as an inmate.
    c. If the person was not married and rented his home (or lived with his parents), then he was taxed as a freeman.

Important: Indentured servants were _not_ taxable. They worked for their masters in order to pay off debts—and, as such, earned no income. Thus, it is not uncommon for men of a taxable age not to appear on colonial tax rolls for up to 3 to 5 years after arrival in this country. Most immigrants who arrived at Philadelphia were of modest means and sold themselves into servitude to pay the cost of passage. Noting when a person first appears on tax rolls may be a clue as to their socioeconomic status upon arrival.

Not all tax lists have survived. The number and years available vary widely from county to county. Some state taxes survive—as well taxes imposed by the British monarch.

The information found on tax lists varies greatly. The following may or may not be included:
   a. Number of acres owned.
   b. Number of livestock owned.
   c. Number of servants and slaves.
   d. Occupation.
   e. Number of persons in the household. (Rare!)
   f. Whether real estate was acquired by warrant, by patent, or by deed.

When I cite tax lists in my research, I either looked at images of the original records or found the information in a trusted source.

Currently, Ancestry.com had images of original taxes records covering most Pennsylvania counties from 1772 to 1789:

Ancestry.com. *Pennsylvania, Tax and Exoneration, 1768-1801* [database on-line]. Provo, UT, USA: Ancestry.com Operations, Inc., 2011.

Original data:
Tax & Exoneration Lists, 1762–1794. Series No. 4.61; Records of the Office of the Comptroller General, RG-4. Pennsylvania Historical & Museum Commission, Harrisburg, Pennsylvania.

The LDS church filmed tax records for most Maryland and Pennsylvania counties. They can be located via the Family Search Catalogue. Also, a number of dedicated researchers have published abstracts of tax records (e.g., Gary T. Hawbaker and Clyde Groff in Lancaster County).

Extant tax lists should be held at the appropriate department at the county court house. Often, early records have been deposited at the county archives or historical society.

Index of Surnames

A

Aible, 55
Albert, 9, 10, 12, 14, 15, 16, 17, 18, 19, 21, 22, 68, 74
Albrecht, 12, 17, 18

B

Balmer, 46, 55
Balmerin, 46
Bauman, 52
Baumann, 52
Becher, 9, 10, 12, 15, 23, 24, 51
Bechtel, 71
Becker, 23, 84
Behme, 61
Beinhauer, 60
Bekle, 49
Beyerle, 19
Bickins, 29, 30
Binkly, 38
Blattenberger, 66
Boehm, 61
Böhme, 59
Boltz, 9, 10, 15, 25, 26, 91
Boltzin, 34
Born, 19, 84
Braun, 9, 10, 15, 27, 28, 39, 40, 69, 74, 90, 91
Britz, 9, 10, 15, 29, 30
Brosius, 18
Brown, 14, 28, 42
Buch, 69
Burckhardt, 75
Burgstahler, 14, 15, 31, 32, 33, 62, 88
Bussard, 47

C

Cammerer, 87
Carpenter, 52
Class, 33

D

Danner, 61
Deiss, 33
Difendorfer, 52
Diller, 52
Dischong, 66
Dishong, 67
Dotter, 59
Dotterer, 61
Dreher, 84
Dreisch, 84

E

Eckhard, 75
Edinger, 63
Egle, 76
Eichelberger, 19, 37, 38, 46, 72
Eichelbergerin, 19
Elser, 9, 10, 13, 15, 34, 36, 37, 38
Elsser, 94

F

Fetter, 43
Fischer, 33, 84
Frantz, 13
Freeman, 47
Friedel, 84
Friedle, 84
Fritz, 90
Fuchs, 55

G

Gangolff, 9, 10
Gangwolff, 3, 15, 39, 40
Gauer, 46
Geckenheimer, 62
Gertner, 43

Gloninger, 67
Grözingen, 82

H

Haberlandin, 55
Hacker, 9, 10, 15, 38, 41, 43, 48, 57, 65
Haeffele, 84
Haehnle, 84
Hag, 60
Hager, 9, 10, 11, 36, 48, 68, 69, 79, 86, 91, 93
Hagerin, 34, 68, 86, 93, 94
Hagger, 28
Hahnle, 83
Hainlin, 83
Hauck, 59
Haushalter, 3, 9, 10, 15, 23, 24, 41, 42, 43, 44, 45, 46, 47, 48, 49, 51, 93
Hausshalter, 24, 45, 46, 49, 60
Heinz, 74
Hens, 65
Hensel, 67
Högie, 37
Hörner, 16, 17, 88
Hornerin, 32, 88
Hottenstein, 18
Huber, 72

J

Jelter, 19
Jelterin, 19
Jock, 9, 10, 15, 18, 23, 24, 41, 44, 51, 52, 53
Jockin, 81

K

Karch, 60, 91
Karchen, 16
Kast, 19
Keller, 13, 15, 42, 54, 55, 77
Kerezinger, 75
Kerlinger, 87
Kern, 76
Killian, 66
King, 95
Kleber, 84
Klein, 76
Klinger, 18
Kock, 82
Konig, 69
Kühner, 17

L

Laber, 52
Lang, 9, 15, 41, 49, 56, 60, 65
Lauberin, 28
Laurie, 55
Lehman, 75
Lehmann, 35, 75
Lehn, 45, 46
Line, 97
Long, 59, 60, 61
Loresch, 84
Lowrey, 55
Lowry, 55
Lutz, 87

M

Maerkel, 60
Maintzer, 16
Martin, 69
Mayer, 67
Mead, 66
Meinser, 66
Miller, 13, 50, 62, 63, 75, 76, 87
Millerin, 38, 60
Mock, 10, 13, 14, 15, 29, 33, 35, 36, 37, 38, 54
Monroe, 98
Montelius, 66
Moog, 51
Mosser, 66
Motz, 46, 72
Muller, 15, 33, 62, 63
Müller, 3, 32, 33, 38, 62, 63
Myer, 18

N

Nagel, 31

Nees, 9, 10, 13, 64, 65, 66, 67, 68, 71
Neess, 12, 15, 17, 56, 57, 64, 65, 68, 69, 71, 93
Neessin, 56, 57, 64
Neff, 9, 10, 17, 68
Ness, 73
Nicholas, 65

O

Oberle, 69
Oberlin, 19, 27, 38, 50, 69, 72, 87
Obold, 44, 45

P

Paulus, 34

R

Reinacher, 9, 10, 16, 17, 19, 23, 39, 68, 91
Renninger, 84
Richards, 61
Rosenbaum, 84
Roth, 9, 10, 85, 88, 91
Rüger, 25, 26

S

Schad, 82
Schmezer, 60
Schmid, 35
Schmidt, 9, 10, 15, 34, 36, 39, 54, 77, 79, 80, 87, 91
Schneider, 23, 76
Schnurer, 46
Schonteler, 73
Schuesseler, 63
Schweichin, 63
Seitz, 9, 10, 14, 15, 22, 27, 28, 74, 75, 76
Seitzin, 28
Seltzer, 33
Shoemaker, 66
Shotter, 66
Snider, 18
Speck, 6, 9, 10, 14, 15, 22, 34, 65, 77, 81, 82, 83, 84
Spickler, 87

Spöck, 93
Stäbler, 43
Stober, 12, 19, 37, 38, 46, 50, 72
Stoever, 38
Stover, 30, 66
Straup, 54
Straussin, 31
Suss, 46
Süss, 19
Süssin, 19

U

Ulmer, 21

W

Wachter, 38
Wächter, 14, 16, 33, 37, 38, 42
Wagner, 33
Weber, 9, 10, 13, 25, 78, 88, 89, 92
Weberin, 32, 88
Wehre, 28
Weidman, 45, 49, 50
Weidmann, 10, 17, 43, 45, 49, 68
Weidtmann, 19
Wentzin, 74
Werner, 21, 29, 64, 65, 66, 85
Wildtfang, 84
Withington, 18
Wittington, 75
Wittman, 42, 45
Wolf, 65
Wolfarth, 37
Wolffssperger, 19

Y

Yock, 52
Yok, 18

Z

Zeller, 19
Zimmerman, 13, 15, 86, 87, 93
Zimmermann, 9, 10, 11, 87, 92

Last updated 25 July 2018.

Copyright 2018, Edward N. Wevodau.

Thank You!

Also: Please be advised that this is a living file and will be subject to future updates and revisions. I welcome any additional information that improves the accuracy and content of this file.